STUDENT UNIT GUIDE

A2 Chemistry
UNIT 2814

OCR

Module 2814: Chains, Rings and Spectroscopy

Mike Smith

A2 Chemistry

Philip Allan Updates
Market Place
Deddington
Oxfordshire
OX15 0SE

tel: 01869 338652
fax: 01869 337590
e-mail: sales@philipallan.co.uk
www.philipallan.co.uk

© Philip Allan Updates 2002

ISBN-13: 978-0-86003-870-2
ISBN-10: 0-86003-870-X

All rights reserved; no part of this publication may be reproduced, stored in a retrieval system, or transmitted, in any form or by any means, electronic, mechanical, photocopying, recording or otherwise without either the prior written permission of Philip Allan Updates or a licence permitting restricted copying in the United Kingdom issued by the Copyright Licensing Agency Ltd, 90 Tottenham Court Road, London W1T 4LP.

This Guide has been written specifically to support students preparing for the OCR A2 Chemistry Unit 2814 examination. The content has been neither approved nor endorsed by OCR and remains the sole responsibility of the author.

Printed by MPG Books, Bodmin

Contents

Introduction
About this guide 4
Study skills and revision techniques 5
Approaching the unit test 8

Content Guidance
About this section 12
Summary of required AS chemistry 13
Arenes 16
Carbonyl compounds 21
Carboxylic acids and esters 26
Stereoisomerism and organic synthesis 30
Nitrogen compounds 34
Polymerisation 38
Spectroscopy 43

Questions and Answers
About this section 50
Q1 Addition polymers 51
Q2 Nitration of arenes 53
Q3 Carbonyls and carboxylic acids 57
Q4 Amino acids 60
Q5 Organic synthesis 63
Q6 Carboxylic acids, esters and aldehydes 66
Q7 Amides, esters and chirality 69
Q8 Basicity and azo dyes 74
Q9 Spectroscopy 77

Introduction

About this guide

This unit guide is written to help you to prepare for Unit Test 2814, which examines the content of **Module 2814: Chains, Rings and Spectroscopy**.

This **Introduction** provides advice on how to use the guide, together with suggestions for effective revision.

The **Content Guidance** section gives a point-by-point description of all the facts you need to know and concepts that you need to understand for Module 2814. It aims to provide you with a basis for your revision. However, you must also be prepared to use other sources in your preparation for the examination.

The **Question and Answer** section shows you the sort of questions you can expect in the unit test. It would be impossible to give examples of every kind of question in one book, but the questions used should give you a flavour of what to expect. Each question has been attempted by two candidates, Candidate A and Candidate B. Their answers, along with the examiner's comments, should help you to see what you need to do to score a good mark — and how you can easily *not* score marks, even though you probably understand the chemistry.

What can I assume about the guide?

You can assume that:
- the topics covered in the Content Guidance section relate directly to those in the specification
- the basic facts you need to know are stated clearly
- the major concepts you need to understand are explained
- the questions at the end of the guide are similar in style to those that will appear in the unit test
- the answers supplied are genuine, combining responses commonly written by candidates
- the standard of the marking is broadly equivalent to the standard that will be applied to your answers

What can I *not* assume about the guide?

You must *not* assume that:
- every last detail has been covered
- the way in which the concepts are explained is the *only* way in which they can be presented in an examination (often concepts are presented in an unfamiliar situation)

- the range of question types presented is exhaustive (examiners are always thinking of new ways to test a topic)

So how should I use this guide?

The guide lends itself to a number of uses throughout your course — it is not *just* a revision aid.

The Content Guidance is laid out in sections that correspond to those of the specification for Module 2814 so that you can:
- use it to check that your notes cover the material required by the specification
- use it to identify strengths and weaknesses
- use it as a reference for homework and internal tests
- use it during your revision to prepare 'bite-sized' chunks of material rather than being faced with a file full of notes

The Question and Answer section can be used to:
- identify the terms used by examiners in questions and what they expect of you
- familiarise yourself with the style of questions you can expect
- identify the ways in which marks are lost or gained

Study skills and revision techniques

All students need to develop good study skills. This section provides advice and guidance on how to study A2 chemistry.

Organising your notes

Chemistry students often accumulate a large quantity of notes, so it is useful to keep these in a well-ordered and logical manner. It is necessary to review your notes regularly, maybe rewriting the notes taken during lessons so that they are clear and concise, with key points highlighted. You should check your notes using textbooks and fill in any gaps. Make sure that you go back and ask your teacher if you are unsure about anything, especially if you find conflicting information in your class notes and textbook.

It is a good idea to file your notes in specification order using a consistent series of headings. The Content Guidance section can help you with this.

Organising your time

When organising your time, make sure that you plan carefully, allowing enough time to cover all of the work. It sounds easy, but it is one of the most difficult things to do. There is considerable evidence to show that revising for 2–3 hours at a time is counter-productive and that it is much better to work in short, sharp bursts of between 30 minutes and an hour.

Preparation for examinations is a very personal thing. Different people prepare, equally successfully, in very different ways. The key is being totally honest about what actually *works for you*.

Whatever your style, you must have a plan. Sitting down the night before the examination with a file full of notes and a textbook does not constitute a revision plan — it is just desperation — and you must not expect a great deal from it. Whatever your personal style, there are a number of things you *must* do and a number of other things you *could* do.

The Chains, Rings and Spectroscopy unit contains new terminology and concepts. There is a large body of factual knowledge, relating to reagents and reaction conditions, which must be learnt.

The scheme outlined below is a suggestion as to how you might revise Module 2814 over a 3-week period. The work pattern shown is fairly simple. It involves revising and/or rewriting a topic and then over the next few days going through it repeatedly but never spending more than 30 minutes at a time. When you are confident that you have covered all areas, start trying to answer questions from past papers or this guide's Question and Answer section. Mark them yourself and seek help with anything that you are not sure about.

Day	Week 1	Week 2	Week 3
Mon	Topic 1 — Arenes Allow about 30 minutes	Topic 7 — 20 minutes Topic 6 — 10 minutes	Using past papers or other question sources, try a structured question on Topic 6 Mark it and list anything you do not understand Allow about 30 minutes
Tue	Topic 2 — Carbonyl compounds Allow about 30 minutes, followed by 10 minutes rereading yesterday's notes on Topic 1	Reread all your summary notes at least twice	Using past papers or other question sources, try a structured question on Topic 7 Mark it and list anything you do not understand Allow about 30 minutes
Wed	Topic 3 — Carboxylic acids and esters Allow about 30 minutes, followed by 10 minutes rereading yesterday's notes on Topic 2 and 5 minutes going over Topic 1	Using past papers or other question sources, try a structured question on Topic 1 Mark it and list anything you do not understand Allow about 30 minutes	You have now revised all of Module 2814 Make a list of your weaknesses and ask your teacher for help Reread all your summary notes at least twice Ask someone to test you

Day	Week 1	Week 2	Week 3
Thu	Topic 4 — Stereoisomerism and organic synthesis Allow about 30 minutes, followed by 10 minutes rereading yesterday's notes on Topic 3, 5 minutes going over Topic 2 and, finally, 2 minutes on Topic 1	Using past papers or other question sources, try a structured question on Topic 2 Mark it and list anything you do not understand Allow about 30 minutes	Using past papers or other question sources, try a relevant question that requires extended writing (essay-type questions) from any of the topics Mark it and list anything you do not understand Allow about 30 minutes
Fri	Topic 5 — Nitrogen compounds Allow about 30 minutes, followed by 10 minutes rereading yesterday's notes on Topic 4, 5 minutes going over Topic 3 and, finally, 2 minutes on Topic 2 By now you should know Topic 1	Using past papers or other question sources, try a structured question on Topic 3 Mark it and list anything you do not understand Allow about 30 minutes	Using past papers or other question sources, try a relevant question that requires extended writing (essay-type questions) from any of the topics Mark it and list anything you do not understand Allow about 30 minutes
Sat	Topic 6 — Polymerisation Allow about 30 minutes, followed by 10 minutes rereading yesterday's notes on Topic 5, 5 minutes going over Topic 4 and, finally, 2 minutes on Topic 3 By now you should know Topics 1 and 2	Using past papers or other question sources, try a structured question on Topic 4 Mark it and list anything you do not understand Allow about 30 minutes	Reread all your summary notes at least twice Concentrate on the weaknesses you identified on Wednesday (by now you should have talked to your teacher about them) Ask someone to test you
Sun	Topic 7 — Spectroscopy Allow about 30 minutes, followed by 10 minutes rereading yesterday's notes on Topic 6, 5 minutes going over Topic 5 and, finally, 2 minutes on Topic 4 By now you should know Topics 1, 2 and 3	Using past papers or other question sources, try a structured question on Topic 5 Mark it and list anything you do not understand Allow about 30 minutes	Attempt a past exam paper Allow 90 minutes Use your notes and other sources to mark your responses List anything you do not understand Plan to see your teacher for additional help with your weaknesses

A2 Chemistry

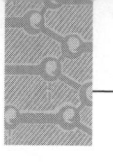

This revision timetable may not suit you, in which case write one to meet your needs. It is only there to give you an idea of how one might work. The most important thing is that the grid at least enables you to see what you should be doing and when you should be doing it. Do not try to be too ambitious — *little and often is by far the best way*.

It would of course be sensible to put together a longer rolling programme to cover all your A2 subjects. Do *not* leave it too late. Start sooner rather than later.

Things you *must* do

- Leave yourself enough time to cover *all* the material.
- Make sure that you actually *have* all the material to hand (use this book as a basis).
- Identify weaknesses early in your preparation so that you have time to do something about them.
- Familiarise yourself with the terminology used in examination questions.

Things you *could* do to help you learn

- Copy selected portions of your notes.
- Write a precis of your notes, which includes all the key points.
- Write key points on postcards (carry them round with you for a quick revise during a coffee break!).
- Discuss a topic with a friend also studying the same course.
- Try to explain a topic to someone *not* on the course.
- Practise examination questions on the topic.

Approaching the unit test

Terms used in the unit test

You will be asked precise questions in the unit test, so you can save a lot of valuable time as well as ensuring you score as many marks as possible by knowing what is expected. Terms used most commonly are explained below.

Define

This requires a precise statement to explain a chemical term. It could involve specific amounts or conditions such as temperature and pressure.

Explain

This normally implies that a definition should be given, together with some relevant comment on the significance or context of the term(s) concerned, especially where two or more terms are included in the question. The amount of supplementary comment should be determined by the mark allocation.

State
This implies a concise answer with little or no supporting argument.

Describe
This requires you to state in words (but using diagrams where appropriate) the main points of the topic. It is often used with reference either to particular phenomena or to particular experiments. In the former instance, the term usually implies that the answer should include reference to observations associated with the phenomena. The amount of description should be determined by the mark allocation. You are not expected to explain the phenomena or experiments, but merely to describe them.

Deduce or predict
This means that you are not expected to produce the answer by recall but by making a logical connection between other pieces of information. Such information may be wholly given in the question or could depend on answers given in an earlier part of the question. 'Predict' also implies a concise answer, with no supporting statement required.

Outline
This implies brevity, i.e. restricting the answer to essential detail only.

Suggest
This is used in two contexts. It implies either that there is no unique answer or that you are expected to apply your knowledge to a 'novel' situation that may not be formally in the specification.

Calculate
This is used when a numerical answer is required. In general, working should be shown.

Sketch
When this is applied to diagrams, it means that a simple, freehand drawing is acceptable. Nevertheless, care should be taken over proportions, and important details should be labelled clearly.

On the day

When you finally open the test paper, it can be quite a stressful moment and you need to be certain of your strategy. The test paper consists of structured questions (usually five or six) and free-response questions (usually one or two). The structured questions usually account for between 70 and 75 marks and the free-response questions are worth 15 to 20 marks. The total number of marks on the paper is 90.

Time will be very tight; there are only 90 minutes for this 90-mark paper. So:
- do *not* begin writing as soon as you open the paper
- scan *all* the questions before you begin to answer any
- identify those questions about which you feel most confident
- *read the question carefully* — if you are asked to explain, then explain, do *not* just describe

- take notice of the mark allocation and do not supply the examiner with all your knowledge of any topic if there is only 1 mark allocated — similarly, you have to come up with *four* ideas if 4 marks are allocated
- try to stick to the point in your answer — it is easy to stray into related areas that will not score marks and will use up valuable time
- try to answer *all* the questions

Structured questions

These are questions that may require a single-word answer, a short sentence or a response amounting to several sentences. The setter for the paper will have thought carefully about the amount of space required for the answer and the marks allocated, so the space provided usually gives a good indication of the amount of detail required.

Free-response questions

These questions enable you to demonstrate the depth and breadth of your knowledge as well as your ability to communicate chemical ideas in a concise way. These questions will often include marks for the quality of written communication. You are expected to use appropriate scientific terminology and to write in continuous prose, paying particular attention to spelling, punctuation and grammar.

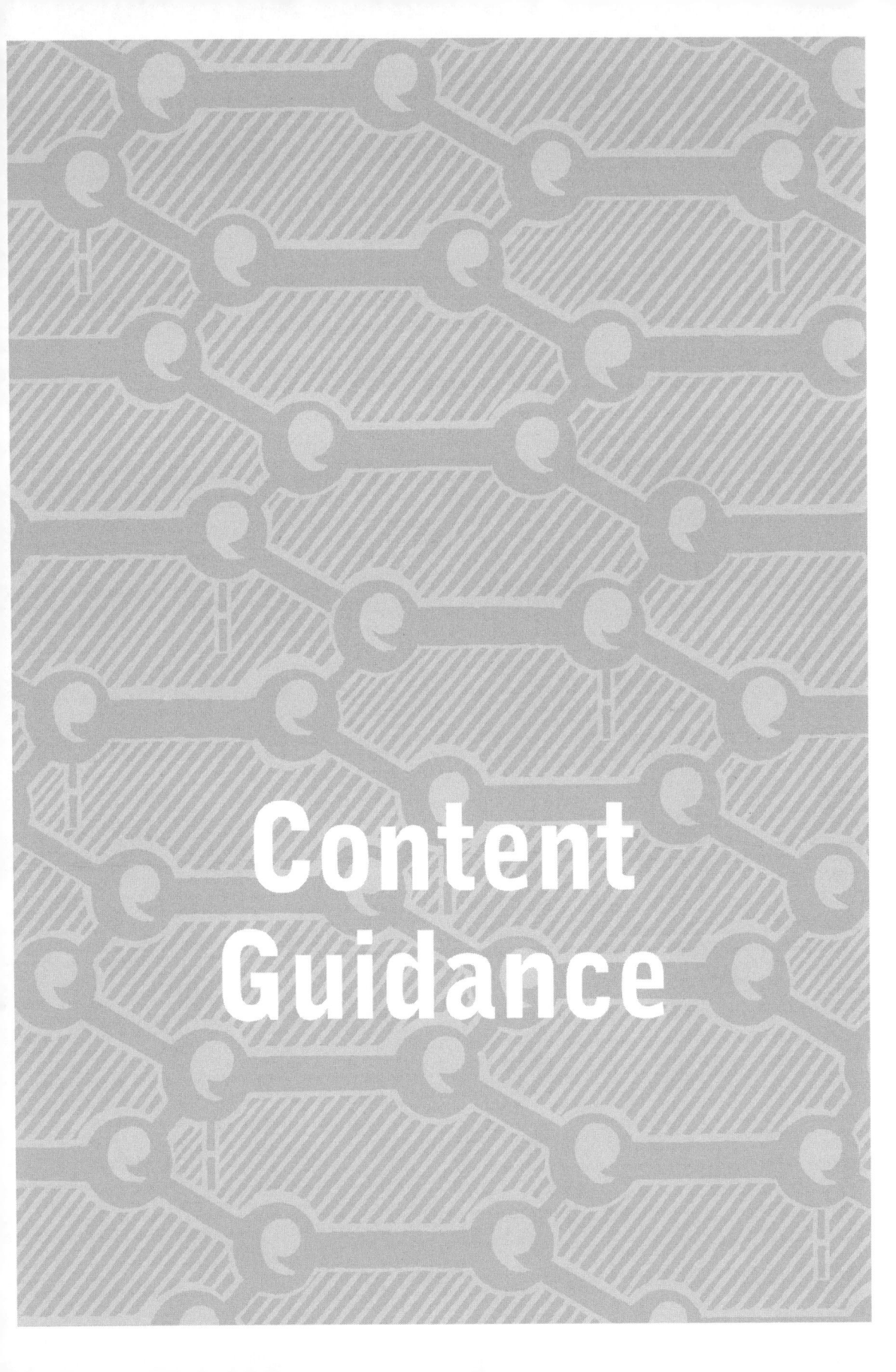

Content Guidance

A2 Chemistry

This Content Guidance section is a student's guide to Module 2814.

The main topics are:
- Arenes
  - the structure of benzene
  - electrophilic substitution reactions
  - phenols
- Carbonyl compounds
  - reactions of aldehydes and ketones
  - oxidation reactions
- Carboxylic acids and esters
  - acidic reactions
  - esterification
  - hydrolysis of esters
- Stereoisomerism and organic synthesis
  - *cis–trans* and optical isomerism
  - two-stage organic synthesis
  - chirality and its importance in pharmaceuticals
- Nitrogen compounds
  - primary amines
  - amino acids
  - hydrolysis of proteins
- Polymerisation
  - addition polymerisation
  - condensation polymerisation
  - uses of polymers
- Spectroscopy
  - mass spectrometry
  - infrared spectroscopy
  - nuclear magnetic resonance spectroscopy

This section includes all the relevant key facts required by the specification and explains the essential concepts.

Summary of required AS chemistry

Module 2814 aims to build upon the concepts developed during the AS course, particularly those in Module 2812: Chains and Rings. You are expected to be able to use the concepts developed at AS; you are *not* expected to recall factual knowledge such as reagents and conditions for specific reactions.

You are expected to recall that organic chemicals can be grouped into homologous series in which each member of the series differs from the next by CH_2. Each member of a homologous series contains a particular group of atoms attached to the carbon chain or ring. This group determines the chemistry of that series and is referred to as the functional group. A general formula can be written for each homologous series.

You need to be able to use displayed formulae, molecular formulae, empirical formulae, structural formulae and skeletal formulae. You should be able name individual chemicals, including structural isomers and *cis–trans* isomers.

Name	Displayed formula	Molecular formula	Empirical formula	Structural formula	Skeletal formula
But-1-ene	H₂C=CH–C₂H₅ (H, H on one C; C₂H₅, H on other)	C_4H_8	CH_2	$CH_3CH_2CHCH_2$	
cis-But-2-ene	H, H on same side; H₃C, CH₃ on same side	C_4H_8	CH_2	$CH_3CHCHCH_3$	
trans-But-2-ene	H, CH₃ opposite; H₃C, H opposite	C_4H_8	CH_2	$CH_3CHCHCH_3$	
Methylpropene	H, CH₃ / H, CH₃ arrangement	C_4H_8	CH_2	$CH_2C(CH_3)_2$	

You are expected to be able to determine empirical formulae and to calculate percentage yield from experimental data.

Terms introduced at AS will be used and it is essential that these are fully understood. These include:

- **free radical** — contains a single unpaired electron (e.g. Cl•)

A2 Chemistry

- **nucleophile** — an electron pair donor (e.g. OH⁻)
- **electrophile** — an electron pair acceptor (e.g. H⁺)

It is unlikely that you will be tested on specific mechanisms met in Module 2812. However, the concept of showing movement of electrons by the use of 'curly arrows' is further developed and it is advisable to revise the three mechanisms encountered in AS organic chemistry. These are:
- **free radical substitution** in reactions between alkanes and halogens
- **electrophilic addition** in reactions between alkenes and halogens
- **nucleophilic substitution** in the hydrolysis of halogenoalkanes

Addition polymerisation was introduced at AS and is studied at greater depth in this A2 unit. Difficult new concepts are introduced, for example tacticity (isotactic, syndiotactic and atactic polymers). It is essential that you understand the basic ideas and can construct relevant polymers from a given monomer. Some common monomers and their corresponding polymers are shown below:

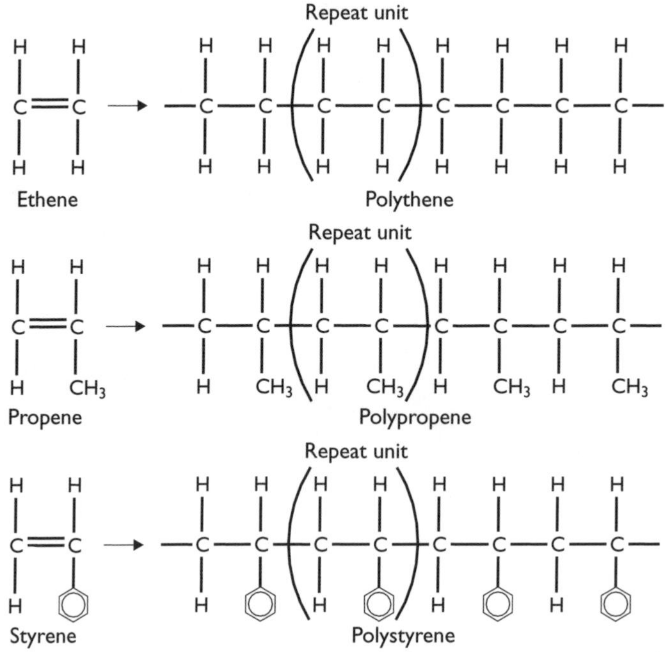

Ethene → Polythene

Propene → Polypropene

Styrene → Polystyrene

The section devoted to alcohols is particularly relevant. The oxidation of alcohols can produce ketones, aldehydes or carboxylic acids. All three functional groups are studied at A2 and it is therefore essential that you can recall suitable equations, reagents and conditions.

Alcohols can be oxidised using acidified dichromate, $Cr_2O_7^{2-}/H^+$ ($K_2Cr_2O_7/H_2SO_4$). This oxidising mixture is bright orange and changes to green during the redox process. When oxidising a primary alcohol, the choice of apparatus is important. Refluxing produces a carboxylic acid; distillation produces an aldehyde. Balanced equations are written for these oxidation reactions using [O] to represent the oxidising agent.

OCR Unit 2814

Oxidation of primary alcohols to **aldehydes**:

$CH_3OH + [O] \longrightarrow HCHO + H_2O$
Methanol   Methanal

$CH_3CH_2OH + [O] \longrightarrow CH_3CHO + H_2O$
Ethanol   Ethanal

Oxidation of secondary alcohols to **ketones**:

$CH_3CHOHCH_3 + [O] \longrightarrow CH_3COCH_3 + H_2O$
Propan-2-ol   Propan-2-one

$CH_3CH_2CHOHCH_3 + [O] \longrightarrow CH_3CH_2COCH_3 + H_2O$
Butan-2-ol   Butan-2-one

Oxidation of primary alcohols to **carboxylic acids**:

$CH_3OH + 2[O] \longrightarrow HCOOH + H_2O$
Methanol   Methanoic acid

$CH_3CH_2OH + 2[O] \longrightarrow CH_3COOH + H_2O$
Ethanol   Ethanoic acid

Alcohols also react with carboxylic acids to produce esters and water. These reactions were studied at AS and are also important at A2.

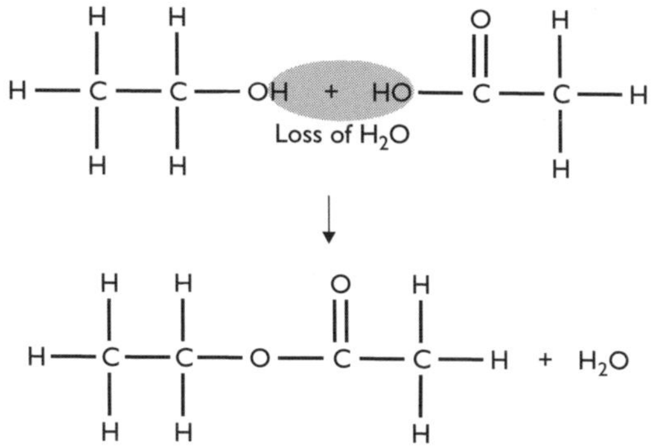

Reactions of ethanol that may be tested at A2 include:

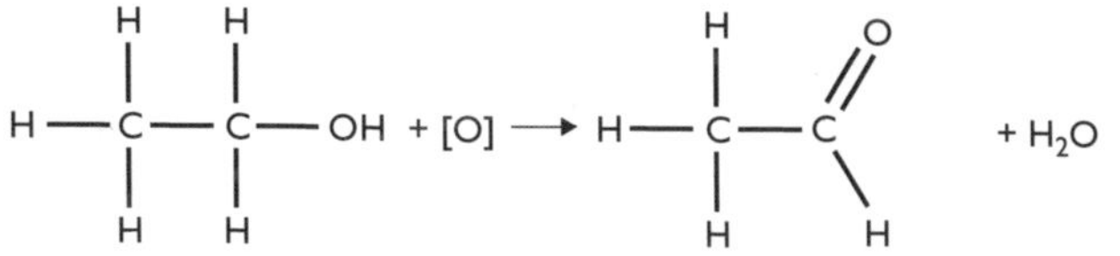

+ H₂O   When distilled

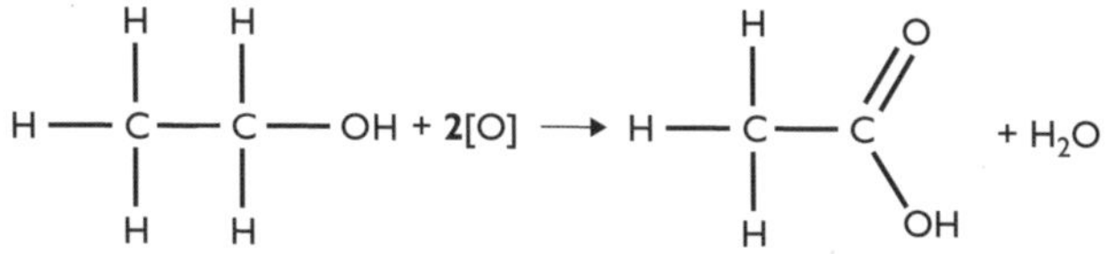

+ H₂O   When refluxed

15

In these cases, the oxidising agent is $H^+/Cr_2O_7^{2-}$ and we see a colour change of orange to green. If the ethanol is set up under reflux, it is completely oxidised to ethanoic acid, but if it is set up under distillation, ethanal can be separated out.

Arenes

The simplest arene is **benzene**. The composition of benzene by mass is C, 92.3%; H, 7.7%. Its relative molecular mass is 78. This information shows that the empirical formula is CH and the molecular formula is C_6H_6.

Structure of benzene

The French chemist August Kekulé suggested that benzene was a cyclic molecule with alternating C=C double bonds and C–C single bonds.

However, there are three major pieces of evidence against this type of structure.
- Compounds that contain C=C double bonds readily decolorise bromine. Benzene only reacts with bromine when boiled and exposed to ultraviolet light. This casts doubt on the existence of C=C double bonds in benzene.
- On average, the length of a C–C single bond is 154 pm while the average length of a C=C double bond is 134 pm. All the bonds in benzene are 139 pm. This suggests an intermediate bond somewhere between a double bond and a single bond.
- Experimentally determined enthalpy changes for cyclohexene and benzene reacting separately with hydrogen give a value for benzene about 150 kJ mol^{-1} less than that expected from the alternating double bond–single bond model.

The current model for benzene takes these observations into account. Each carbon atom contributes one electron to a π-delocalised ring of electrons above and below the plane of atoms. Each carbon has one *p*-orbital at right angles to the plane of atoms.

Each of the *p*-orbitals overlaps with adjacent *p*-orbitals, so that delocalisation is extended over all six carbon atoms.

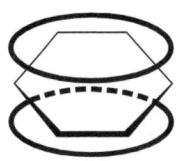

π-delocalised ring above and below the plane

The π-delocalised ring accounts for the increased stability of benzene as well as explaining the reluctance to react with bromine. In addition, it also explains why all six carbon–carbon bond lengths are identical. Benzene is usually represented by the skeletal formula shown below:

Electrophilic substitution

As a result of the presence of the π-delocalised ring, benzene is very stable. However, benzene does react with electrophiles that have a full positive charge — an induced dipole in a molecule is not normally sufficient.

An electrophile is defined as a electron pair acceptor. The most used electrophile is H^+ and it is clearly pointless reacting benzene, C_6H_6, with H^+. Catalysts are required to generate electrophiles such as NO_2^+, Cl^+, Br^+ and CH_3^+. The general equation for this is:

$$C_6H_6 + X^+ \longrightarrow C_6H_5X + H^+$$

where X^+ is the electrophile.

Nitration of benzene
Reagents: HNO_3 and H_2SO_4 (catalyst)
Conditions: approximately 60 °C
Balanced equation: $C_6H_6 + HNO_3 \longrightarrow C_6H_5NO_2 + H_2O$
Mechanism:
- Generation of the electrophile:

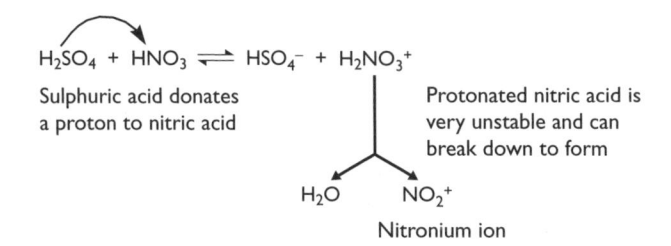

$$H_2SO_4 + HNO_3 \rightleftharpoons HSO_4^- + H_2NO_3^+$$

Sulphuric acid donates a proton to nitric acid

Protonated nitric acid is very unstable and can break down to form

H_2O NO_2^+

Nitronium ion

- Electrophilic attack at the benzene ring:

- Regeneration of the catalyst:
  $H^+ + HSO_4^- \longrightarrow H_2SO_4$

Halogenation of benzene
Reagents: Cl_2 and $AlCl_3$ (catalyst)
Conditions: anhydrous
Balanced equation: $C_6H_6 + Cl_2 \longrightarrow C_6H_5Cl + HCl$
Mechanism:
- Generation of the electrophile:
  $Cl_2 + AlCl_3 \longrightarrow Cl^+ + AlCl_4^-$
- Electrophilic attack at the benzene ring:

- Regeneration of the catalyst:
  $H^+ + AlCl_4^- \longrightarrow AlCl_3 + HCl$

The chlorination of benzene is referred to as a Friedel–Crafts reaction in which $AlCl_3$ behaves as a halogen carrier. Halogen carriers are able to accept a halide ion and to 'carry it' through the reaction. At the end of the reaction, the halide ion is released and the hydrogen halide is formed. All aluminium halides, iron(III) halides and iron can behave as halogen carriers.

Bromination of alkenes and arenes
You will recall from Module 2812 that alkenes, for example cyclohexene, react readily with bromine in the absence of sunlight, undergoing electrophilic addition reactions.

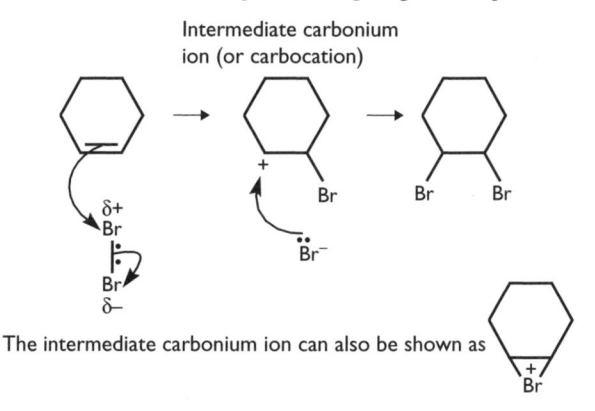

The intermediate carbonium ion can also be shown as

The reaction is rapid and is initiated by the induced dipole in bromine.

Benzene also reacts with bromine but is more resistant, reacting less readily than alkenes, such as cyclohexene. Benzene requires an electrophile with a full positive charge, Br⁺, which is generated in the presence of a halogen carrier. The resultant reaction is electrophilic substitution, *not* electrophilic addition. This is explained by the stability of the π-delocalised ring of electrons that is retained in most reactions of arenes.

Uses of arenes

Arenes such as benzene, methylbenzene and 1,4-dimethylbenzene are used as additives to improve the performance of petrol. They are manufactured by reforming straight-chain alkanes. This topic was covered in Module 2812.

Benzene is the feedstock for a variety of products ranging from medicines, such as aspirin and benzocaine, to explosives such as 2,4,6-trinitromethylbenzene (TNT) and including a range of azo dyes. Phenylethene (styrene) is also manufactured from benzene and is the monomer used to produce the polymer poly(phenylethene) or polystyrene.

Products made from benzene are of great value. However, benzene itself is carcinogenic and may cause leukaemia. Chlorinated benzene compounds are extremely toxic.

Phenols

In phenols, the –OH group is attached directly to the benzene ring.

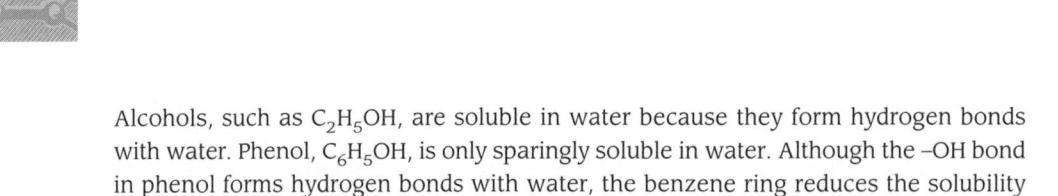

Alcohols, such as C_2H_5OH, are soluble in water because they form hydrogen bonds with water. Phenol, C_6H_5OH, is only sparingly soluble in water. Although the –OH bond in phenol forms hydrogen bonds with water, the benzene ring reduces the solubility because it forms van der Waals forces with neighbouring phenol molecules.

Phenols are weak acids but alcohols are not acidic — ethanol ionises less than water. This difference in acidity can be explained by the relative inductive effect of the aryl and alkyl groups and the relative stability of the phenoxide and ethoxide ions.

The inductive effect can be regarded as the movement of electrons along a σ-bond. It is caused by differences in electronegativities and electron densities. Alkyl groups, such as methyl and ethyl, release electrons along the σ-bond and have a positive inductive effect. In ethanol, this increases the electron density in the O–H bond and so ethanol is unlikely to donate a proton. Additionally, the ethoxide ion is made unstable because the positive inductive effect pushes electrons towards the oxygen, making it more likely to accept a proton.

The benzene ring, C_6H_5-, pulls electrons into the ring and is described as having a negative inductive effect. This weakens the O–H bond in phenol and stabilises the phenoxide ion. It also activates the ring particularly at the 2, 4 and 6 positions. Consequently, phenol behaves as a weak acid and undergoes electrophilic substitution reactions much more readily than benzene.

Phenol forms salts by its reactions with NaOH and Na.

$C_6H_5OH + NaOH \longrightarrow C_6H_5O^-Na^+ + H_2O$

$C_6H_5OH + Na \longrightarrow C_6H_5O^-Na^+ + \frac{1}{2}H_2$

Phenol reacts readily with bromine. The bromine is decolorised and white crystals of 2,4,6-tribromophenol are formed.

Unlike benzene, phenol does not require a halogen carrier and reacts instantly with bromine. This is explained by the activation of the ring due to delocalisation of the lone pairs of electrons on the oxygen atom into the ring. This increases the electron density which in turn polarises the halogen and increases the attraction for the halogen, both of which result in increased reactivity.

Uses of phenols

In the mid-nineteenth century, Lister used a dilute aqueous solution of phenol as an antiseptic. Nowadays, chlorophenols such as 2,4,6-trichlorophenol, TCP, are widely used as antiseptics and disinfectants.

Carbonyl compounds

The presence of the carbonyl group, C=O, in a molecule means that it is unsaturated. The position of the C=O on the carbon chain determines whether or not the compound is classified as an aldehyde or a ketone. Aldehydes always have the C=O at the end of the carbon chain.

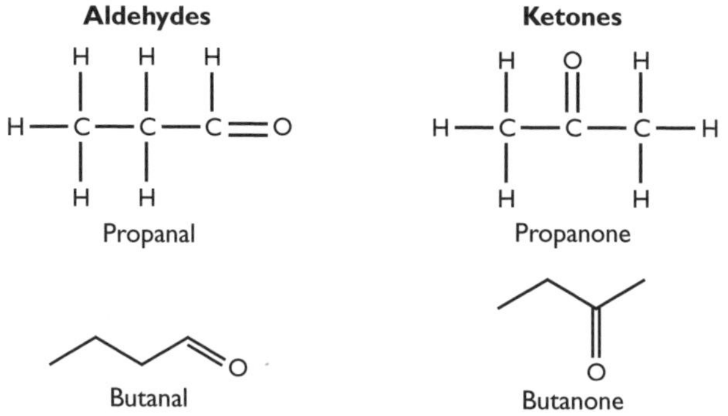

Aldehydes

Propanal

Butanal

Ketones

Propanone

Butanone

You met the carbonyl group in Module 2812 when you studied the chemistry of alcohols. Aldehydes are formed in the first stage of oxidation of primary alcohols; ketones are formed when secondary alcohols are oxidised.

Reactions common to both aldehydes and ketones

Reduction
Aldehydes and ketones can be reduced to their respective alcohols. Sodium tetrahydridoborate(III), $NaBH_4$, is a suitable reducing agent. [H] is used to represent the reducing agent in equations representing organic reduction reactions.

Aldehydes are reduced to **primary alcohols**.
$$CH_3CH_2CHO + 2[H] \longrightarrow CH_3CH_2CH_2OH$$

Ketones are reduced to **secondary alcohols**.
$$CH_3COCH_3 + 2[H] \longrightarrow CH_3CH(OH)CH_3$$

Nucleophilic addition reactions
The carbonyl group is unsaturated and polar and consequently undergoes nucleophilic addition reactions.

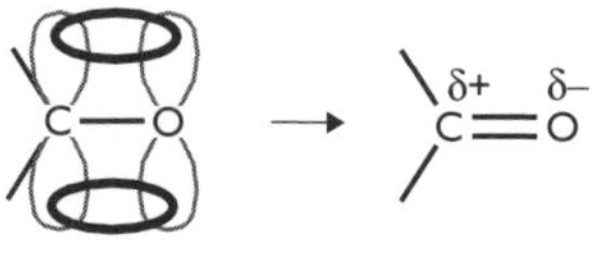

The p-orbitals overlap to form a π-bond

This is best illustrated by the addition reactions with hydrogen cyanide. When describing this mechanism, you should show the movement of electrons by using curly arrows. You should also include relevant dipoles and lone pairs of electrons.

Hydrogen cyanide, HCN, and cyanide ions, $^-$CN, are extremely toxic; experiments involving either should not be performed. Hydrogen cyanide is a covalent gas and therefore has a very low concentration of cyanide ions. It is usual to obtain the $^-$CN ion from potassium cyanide. The $^-$CN ion behaves as the nucleophile and is involved in the initial attack on the carbonyl group. The intermediate anion reacts with a molecule of HCN to form the organic product and generates a cyanide ion, $^-$CN, to continue the reaction.

Propanal and HCN

Propanone and HCN

Reactions with 2,4-dinitrophenylhydrazine

Aldehydes and ketones react with 2,4-dinitrophenylhydrazine (2,4-DNPH) to produce distinctive precipitates. The precipitates are usually bright red, orange or yellow. The reaction between an aldehyde or a ketone with 2,4-DNPH can be used to confirm the presence of a carbonyl compound. The test is very simple and requires adding a few drops of the carbonyl to an excess of 2,4-DNPH — usually about 5 cm³. Although candidates are not expected to recall the formula of 2,4-dinitrophenylhydrazine (the abbreviation 2,4-DNPH is acceptable), it is useful to use it to illustrate the reactions of aldehydes and ketones.

Propanal and 2,4-dinitrophenylhydrazine

Propanal + 2,4-DNPH → 2,4-DNPH derivative of propanal (Orange precipitate) + H$_2$O

Condensation of water

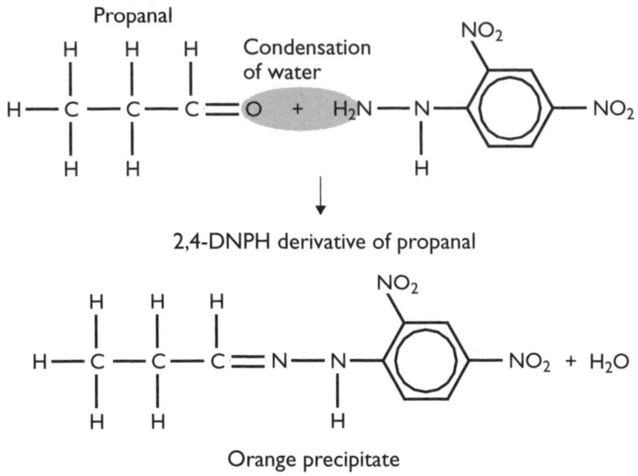

Propanone and 2,4-dinitrophenylhydrazine

Propanone + 2,4-DNPH → 2,4-DNPH derivative of propanone (Orange precipitate) + H$_2$O

Condensation of water

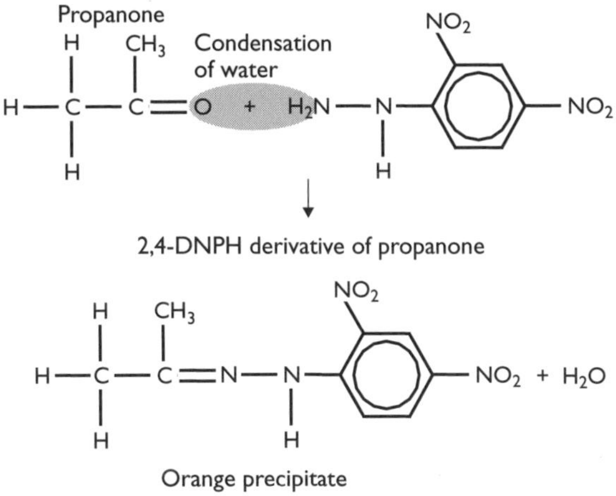

The reactions with 2,4-dinitrophenylhydrazine (2,4-DNPH) are important for two reasons:
- 2,4-DNPH reacts with a carbonyl to produce a distinctively coloured precipitate, which is usually bright red, orange or yellow. Therefore, this reaction can be used to show the presence of a carbonyl group.
- The organic product (the 2,4-DNPH derivative) is relatively easy to purify by re-crystallisation. Therefore, the melting point of the brightly coloured precipitate can be measured. Each derivative has a different melting point, the value of which can be used to identify the specific carbonyl compound. The table below shows the melting points of the derivatives of a few common carbonyl compounds.

Carbonyl compound	Melting point of the 2,4-DNPH derivative/°C
Ethanal	142–143
2-Methylpropanal	180–181
Butanone	109–110
3-Methylbutan-2-one	119–120

Reactions of aldehydes alone

Aldehydes and ketones can be distinguished by a series of redox reactions. Aldehydes are readily oxidised to carboxylic acids whereas ketones are not easily oxidised.

There are three common oxidising mixtures that can be used.

Oxidising mixture	Conditions	Observation
Acidified dichromate, $H^+/Cr_2O_7^{2-}$	Reflux	Colour change from orange to green
Alkaline solution of Cu^{2+} ions (Fehling's solution)	Warm gently in a water bath at about 60 °C	Red precipitate of Cu_2O
Aqueous solution of Ag^+ ions in an excess of ammonia, $Ag(NH_3)_2^+$ (Tollen's reagent)	Warm gently in a water bath at about 60 °C	Ag metal is precipitated and forms a silver mirror

The OCR specification recommends the use of Tollen's reagent to distinguish between aldehydes and ketones. With aldehydes, the Ag^+ ions are reduced to silver metal and the aldehyde is oxidised to a carboxylic acid. The reaction with ethanal is given below:

The Ag^+ ion gains an electron and is, therefore, reduced to silver

$$Ag^+ + e^- \xrightarrow{\text{Reduction}} Ag \text{ (silver mirror)}$$

The aldehyde is oxidised to a carboxylic acid

$$H_3C-CHO + [O] \xrightarrow{\text{Oxidation}} H_3C-COOH$$

Tollen's reagent does not react with ketones because ketones are not oxidised.

OCR Unit 2814

The oxidation of an aldehyde to a carboxylic acid can be followed using infrared spectroscopy, which was first introduced in Module 2812.

Group	Compounds	IR absorption
C=O	Aldehydes, ketones, carboxylic acids	1680–1750 cm^{-1}
O–H	Carboxylic acids	2500–3300 cm^{-1}

The absorption due to the carbonyl group can be seen in the IR spectrum of ethanal.

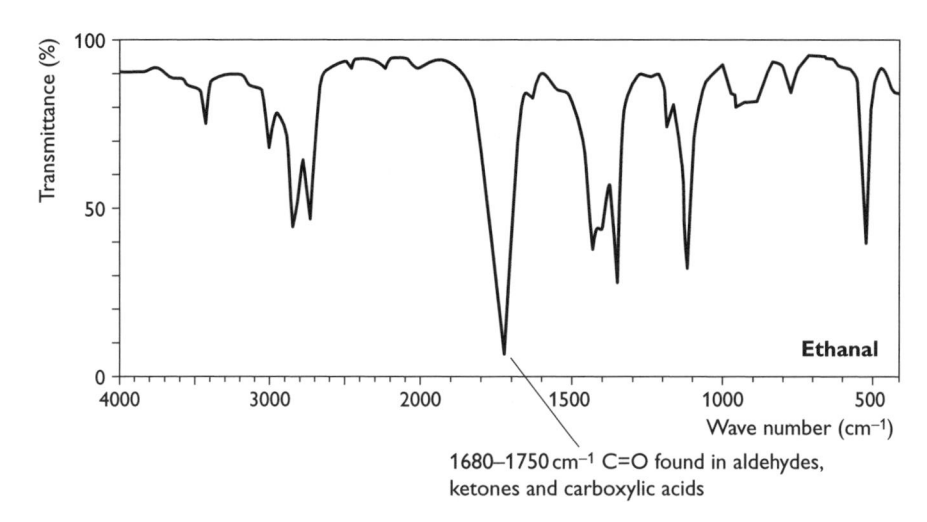

Ethanal

1680–1750 cm^{-1} C=O found in aldehydes, ketones and carboxylic acids

The spectrum below shows the absorption for both the C=O and the O–H groups, confirming that the ethanal has been oxidised to ethanoic acid.

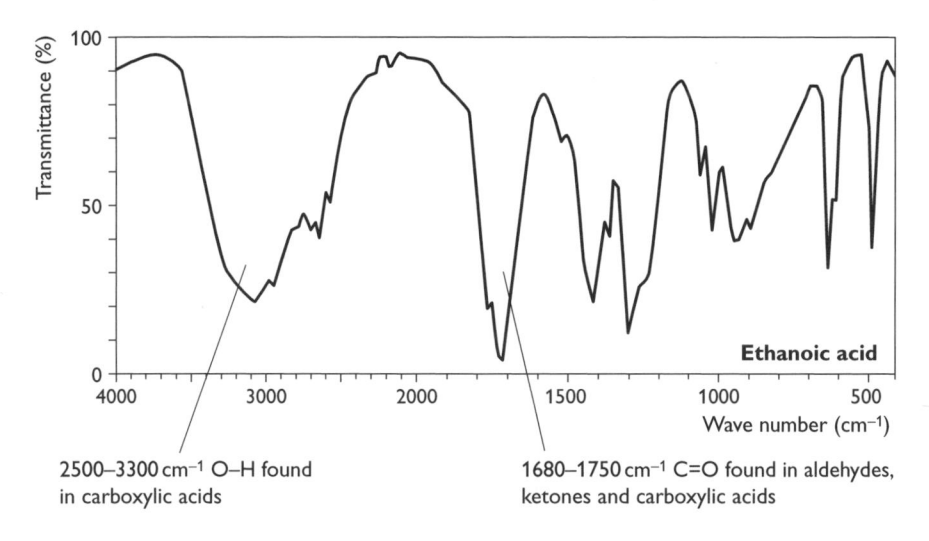

Ethanoic acid

2500–3300 cm^{-1} O–H found in carboxylic acids

1680–1750 cm^{-1} C=O found in aldehydes, ketones and carboxylic acids

A2 Chemistry

Carboxylic acids and esters

All carboxylic acids contain the functional group:

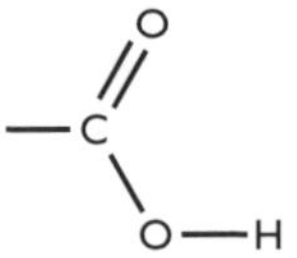

$$-C(=O)-O-H$$

Carboxylic acids are weak acids. They can donate protons but they only partially dissociate into their ions.

$$CH_3CO_2H(aq) \rightleftharpoons CH_3CO_2^-(aq) + H^+(aq)$$

The carboxylic acid group can be attached either to a chain (aliphatic) or to a ring (aromatic). For example:

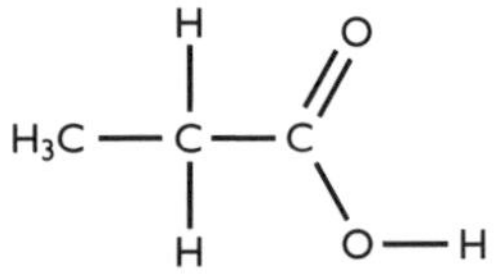

Propanoic acid 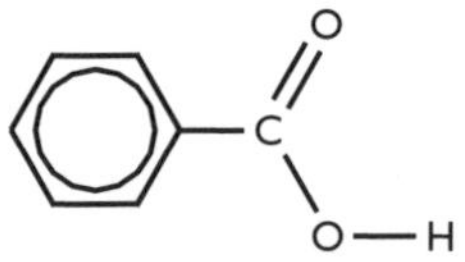   Benzoic acid

Carboxylic acids display typical reactions of an acid and form salts (carboxylates). Salt formation can occur by any of the following reactions:

- acid + base ⟶ salt + water
  $$CH_3CO_2H(aq) + NaOH(aq) \rightarrow CH_3CO_2^-Na^+(aq) + H_2O(l)$$
  ethanoic acid   sodium ethanoate

- acid + (reactive) metal ⟶ salt + water
  $$CH_3CO_2H(aq) + Na(s) \rightarrow CH_3CO_2^-Na^+(aq) + \tfrac{1}{2}H_2(g)$$
  ethanoic acid   sodium ethanoate

- acid + carbonate ⟶ salt + water + carbon dioxide
  $$CH_3CO_2H(aq) + Na_2CO_3(aq) \rightarrow CH_3CO_2^-Na^+(aq) + H_2O(l) + CO_2(g)$$
  ethanoic acid   sodium ethanoate

The reaction with a carbonate can be used as a test for a carboxylic acid. When an acid is added to a solution of a carbonate, bubbles (effervescence) of carbon dioxide are seen.

Carboxylic acids also react with alcohols to form esters. This type of reaction is known as **esterification**. It is reversible and is usually carried out in the presence of an acid catalyst such as sulphuric acid. The general reaction can be summarised as follows:

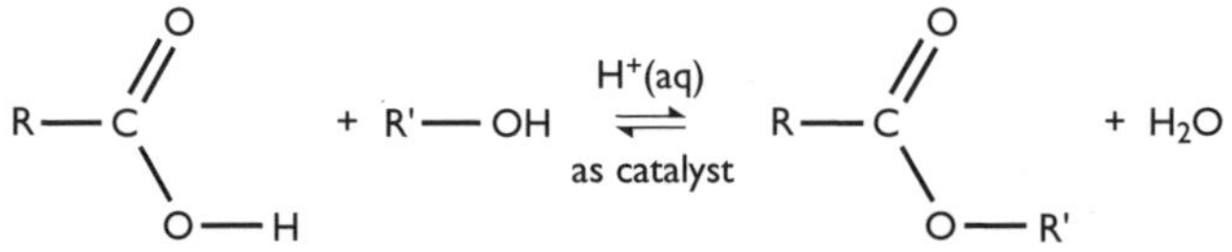

$$R-C(=O)-O-H + R'-OH \underset{\text{as catalyst}}{\overset{H^+(aq)}{\rightleftharpoons}} R-C(=O)-O-R' + H_2O$$

Carboxylic acid   Alcohol   Ester   Water

Esters are named from the alcohol and the carboxylic acid from which they are derived. The first part of the name relates to the alcohol and the second part of the name to the acid. For example:

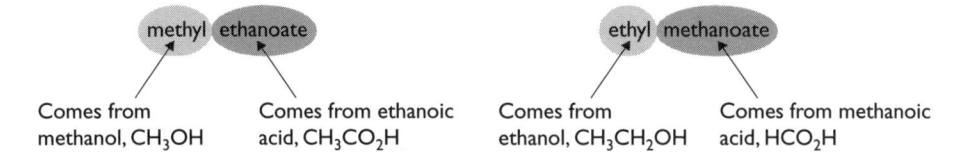

methyl ethanoate

Comes from methanol, CH_3OH
Comes from ethanoic acid, CH_3CO_2H

ethyl methanoate

Comes from ethanol, CH_3CH_2OH
Comes from methanoic acid, HCO_2H

When organic compounds react, the reaction usually occurs between the two functional groups, in this case the alcohol and the carboxylic acid. It is helpful to draw the two reacting molecules with the functional groups facing each other.

The two functional groups react to form water and the ester

$$R-COOH + H-O-R' \underset{\text{as catalyst}}{\overset{H^+(aq)}{\rightleftharpoons}} R-COO-R' + H_2O$$

Carboxylic acid   Alcohol   Ester   Water

For example:

$$H_3C-COOH + H-O-CH_3 \underset{\text{as catalyst}}{\overset{H^+(aq)}{\rightleftharpoons}} H_3C-COO-CH_3 + H_2O$$

Ethanoic acid   Methanol   Methyl ethanoate   Water

$$H-COOH + H-O-C_2H_5 \underset{\text{as catalyst}}{\overset{H^+(aq)}{\rightleftharpoons}} H-COO-C_2H_5 + H_2O$$

Methanoic acid   Ethanol   Ethyl methanoate   Water

Esters are used in flavourings and perfumes. They often contribute to the flavour of fruits.

Fruit	Ester
Banana	1-Methylbutyl ethanoate
Pineapple	Butyl butanoate
Pear	3-Methylbutyl ethanoate
Apple	Ethyl 2-methylbutanoate

A2 Chemistry

Task Draw the structures of the esters that contribute to the fruits listed in the table. The first one is done for you. Remember the first part of the name identifies the alcohol and the second part of the name identifies the carboxylic acid.

$$\text{Ethanoate: } H_3C-C(=O)-O- \quad \text{1-Methylbutyl: } -CH(CH_3)-CH_2-CH_2-CH_3$$

The answers are on page 29.

Esters react with water. The **hydrolysis** reaction is slow and is carried out in the presence of an acid, H⁺(aq), or a base, OH⁻(aq). Acid-catalysed hydrolysis leads to the formation of the carboxylic acid and the alcohol.

$$H_3C-COO-CH_3 + H_2O \underset{\text{as catalyst}}{\overset{H^+(aq)}{\rightleftharpoons}} H_3C-COOH + H-O-CH_3$$

Methyl ethanoate + Water ⇌ Ethanoic acid + Methanol

Base-catalysed hydrolysis leads to the formation of the salt of the carboxylic acid (the carboxylate) and the alcohol.

$$H_3C-COO-CH_3 + H_2O \underset{\text{as catalyst}}{\overset{OH^-(aq)}{\rightleftharpoons}} H_3C-COOH + H-O-CH_3$$

Methyl ethanoate + Water ⇌ Ethanoic acid + Methanol

The carboxylic acid then reacts with the base catalyst

$$H_3C-COO^- Na^+$$

Sodium ethanoate

Fats and oils are naturally occurring esters called **triglycerides**. They can be hydrolysed by refluxing with a base. The products are propane-1,2,3-triol and the salts of the fatty acids. This process is known as **saponification**, which means 'the forming of soap'. Modern soaps are made from blends of oils. The base hydrolysis of a triglyceride is shown below:

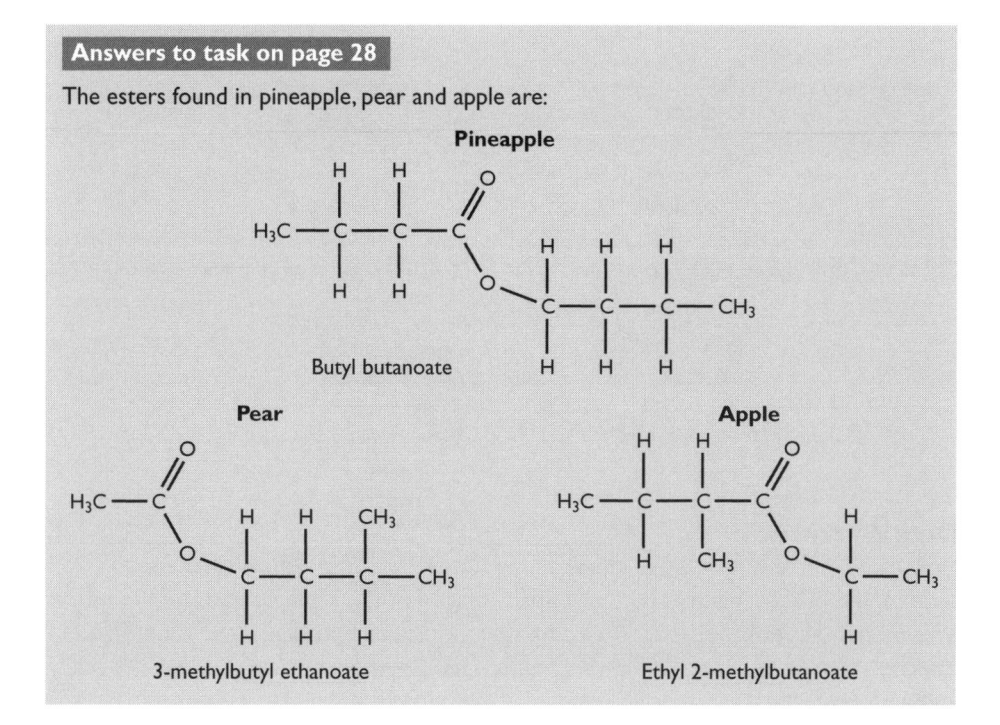

$$CH_3(CH_2)_{16}-\overset{O}{\underset{\|}{C}}-O-\overset{H}{\underset{|}{C}}-H$$

with the glycerol backbone bearing:
- top: $H-\overset{H}{\underset{|}{C}}-O-\overset{O}{\underset{\|}{C}}-(CH_2)_{16}CH_3$
- bottom: $H-\overset{H}{\underset{|}{C}}-O-\overset{O}{\underset{\|}{C}}-(CH_2)_{16}CH_3$

Base hydrolysis ↓

$$\begin{array}{c} H-\overset{H}{\underset{|}{C}}-OH \\ HO-\overset{|}{\underset{|}{C}}-H \\ H-\overset{|}{\underset{H}{C}}-OH \end{array} \;+\; 3\; CH_3(CH_2)_{16}-\overset{O}{\underset{\|}{C}}-O^-Na^+$$

Answers to task on page 28

The esters found in pineapple, pear and apple are:

Pineapple

$H_3C-CH_2-CH_2-C(=O)-O-CH_2-CH_2-CH_2-CH_3$

Butyl butanoate

Pear

$H_3C-C(=O)-O-CH_2-CH_2-CH(CH_3)-CH_3$

3-methylbutyl ethanoate

Apple

$H_3C-CH_2-CH(CH_3)-C(=O)-O-CH_2-CH_3$

Ethyl 2-methylbutanoate

Stereoisomerism and organic synthesis

Stereoisomerism

Stereoisomers are compounds that have the same molecular and structural formulae but have different three-dimensional shapes. There are two kinds of stereoisomerism: *cis–trans* isomerism and optical isomerism.

cis–trans isomerism

cis–trans isomerism is found in alkenes. The key features to look for are:
- the C=C double bond
- each carbon in the C=C double bond attached to two different atoms or groups

There is restricted rotation about the C=C double bond. The different atoms or groups attached to each carbon atom ensure that there is no symmetry around the carbons in the C=C double bond.

But-1-ene and but-2-ene both have a C=C double bond. However, the right-hand carbon in the C=C double bond in but-1-ene is bonded to two hydrogen atoms and butene-1-ene therefore does not exhibit *cis–trans* isomerism.

But-1-ene

But-2-ene

But-2-ene possesses both essential key features and hence has *cis* and *trans* isomers.

cis-But-2-ene

trans-But-2-ene

Optical isomerism

Optical isomerism occurs in **chiral** compounds. A chiral compound contains an asymmetric atom. This means that mirror images of the molecule are non-identical and are **non-superimposable**. The commonest chiral compounds have a carbon atom attached to *four different* atoms or groups. The asymmetric carbon atom is usually shown by an asterisk (*).

OCR Unit 2814

                    CO₂H   CO₂H
                     | |
              H₃C—C*---OH   HO---*C—CH₃
                     | |
                     H   H
                           Mirror

Optical isomers are so called because they behave differently in the presence of plane-polarised light. One isomer rotates the plane-polarised light to the right and the other rotates it to the left. They are said to be optically active.

The preparation of a single chiral compound in the laboratory is extremely difficult — usually an equal amount of each optical isomer is formed. The synthetic mixture contains 50% of the isomer that rotates plane-polarised light to the right and 50% of the isomer that rotates plane-polarised light to the left. Therefore, the synthetic mixture does not rotate plane-polarised light, i.e. it is optically inactive. It is called a **racemic** mixture.

By contrast, naturally occurring chiral compounds produced in living systems often occur as one optical isomer only. In most living things, the amino acids are optical isomers that rotate plane-polarised light to the left — L-amino acids. Often, the two optical isomers behave differently in living systems.

Natural and synthetic medicines often contain chiral molecules; generally, one of the optical isomers is beneficial while the other is not and may have undesirable side effects. In the 1960s, thalidomide was widely prescribed by doctors as a sedative. Sadly, it was discovered that thalidomide could harm babies if taken by mothers during the early months of pregnancy. Thalidomide is a chiral compound; one form is an effective sedative, while the other form causes malformations in babies.

Since the thalidomide affair, the pharmaceutical and agrochemical industries have been required to test both mirror image forms of all chiral compounds separately before they can be used as drugs or agrochemicals. Generally, the beneficial isomer has the appropriate shape to interact with the receptor molecules and chemists are now producing medicines containing single isomers rather than racemic mixtures. This has the effect of increasing pharmacological/agrochemical activity as well as reducing the risk of adverse side effects. The increased pharmacological activity also means that the dosage can be reduced. It is impossible completely to eliminate the possibility of adverse side effects but the production of a single optical isomer reduces the risks greatly.

Organic synthesis

Some organic syntheses can be accomplished by a single reaction, such as the conversion of ethanal to ethanoic acid and of ethanoic acid to ethyl ethanoate.

However, many others cannot be accomplished in a single step. The flow chart below links together the functional groups covered so far in this unit and gives essential reagents and conditions for the reactions. Flow charts like this are a useful way of revising.

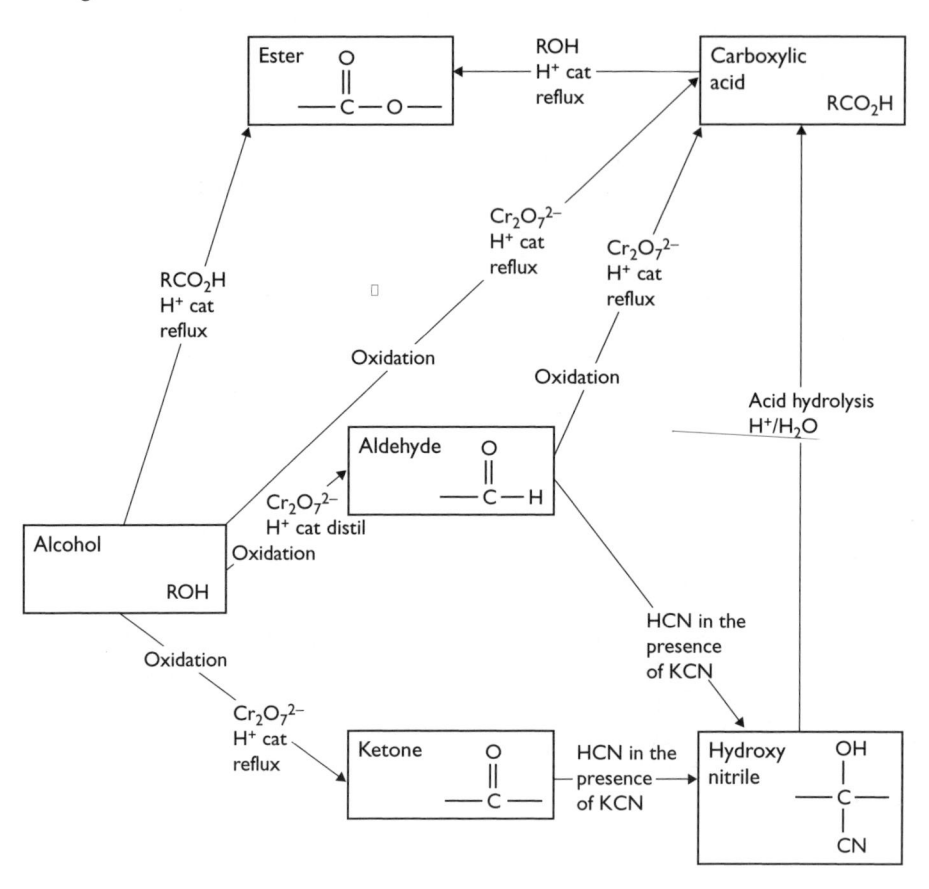

```
                      ROH
   Ester    O      H⁺ cat          Carboxylic
           ‖      ◄────────         acid
          —C—O—    reflux          ────────►   RCO₂H
            ▲                         ▲
            │                         │
            │         Cr₂O₇²⁻         │
            │         H⁺ cat     Cr₂O₇²⁻
            │         reflux      H⁺ cat
   RCO₂H    │                     reflux
   H⁺ cat   │
   reflux   │        Oxidation        │
            │                         │      Oxidation
            │     Aldehyde    O                        Acid hydrolysis
            │                ‖                          H⁺/H₂O
            │               —C—H
            │    Cr₂O₇²⁻
            │    H⁺ cat distil
   Alcohol  │    Oxidation
            │
            ROH
                                           HCN in the
                                           presence
   Oxidation                               of KCN

            Cr₂O₇²⁻
            H⁺ cat    Ketone    O       HCN in the   Hydroxy      OH
            reflux             ‖        presence ──► nitrile       │
                              —C—       of KCN                    —C—
                                                                   │
                                                                   CN
```

Task Copy out the grid and, starting with ethanol, insert all the connections. You should draw out the organic products and identify the reagents and the conditions. The completed flow chart is shown on page 33.

The OCR specification states that you should be able to describe the two-stage synthesis of 2-hydroxypropanoic acid (lactic acid) starting from ethanal. The organic reagent, ethanal, contains two carbon atoms but the organic product, 2-hydroxypropanoic acid, contains three carbon atoms. Hydroxy nitrile compounds are often used as intermediates in two-stage syntheses, as a means of increasing the number of carbon atoms in a molecule. This two-stage synthesis is outlined below:

```
Aldehyde     HCN      Hydroxy     + 2H₂O         Hydroxy
or ketone  ────────►  nitrile   ──────────►     carboxylic    + NH₃
                                 Reflux with      acid
                                  HCl(aq)
```

Aldehyde

$$H-\underset{\underset{H}{|}}{\overset{\overset{H}{|}}{C}}-\overset{\overset{O}{\|}}{C}-H \xrightarrow{HCN} H-\underset{\underset{H}{|}}{\overset{\overset{H}{|}}{C}}-\underset{\underset{H}{|}}{\overset{\overset{OH}{|}}{C}}-CN \xrightarrow[\text{Reflux with HCl(aq)}]{+2H_2O} H-\underset{\underset{H}{|}}{\overset{\overset{H}{|}}{C}}-\underset{\underset{H}{|}}{\overset{\overset{OH}{|}}{C}}-CO_2H + NH_3$$

Ketone

$$H-\underset{\underset{H}{|}}{\overset{\overset{H}{|}}{C}}-\overset{\overset{O}{\|}}{\underset{\underset{CH_3}{|}}{C}} \xrightarrow{HCN} H-\underset{\underset{H}{|}}{\overset{\overset{H}{|}}{C}}-\underset{\underset{CH_3}{|}}{\overset{\overset{OH}{|}}{C}}-CN \xrightarrow[\text{Reflux with HCl(aq)}]{+2H_2O} H-\underset{\underset{H}{|}}{\overset{\overset{H}{|}}{C}}-\underset{\underset{CH_3}{|}}{\overset{\overset{OH}{|}}{C}}-CO_2H + NH_3$$

The NH$_3$ produced reacts with the acid catalyst (HCl) to produce ammonium chloride.

$$NH_3 + HCl \longrightarrow NH_4Cl$$

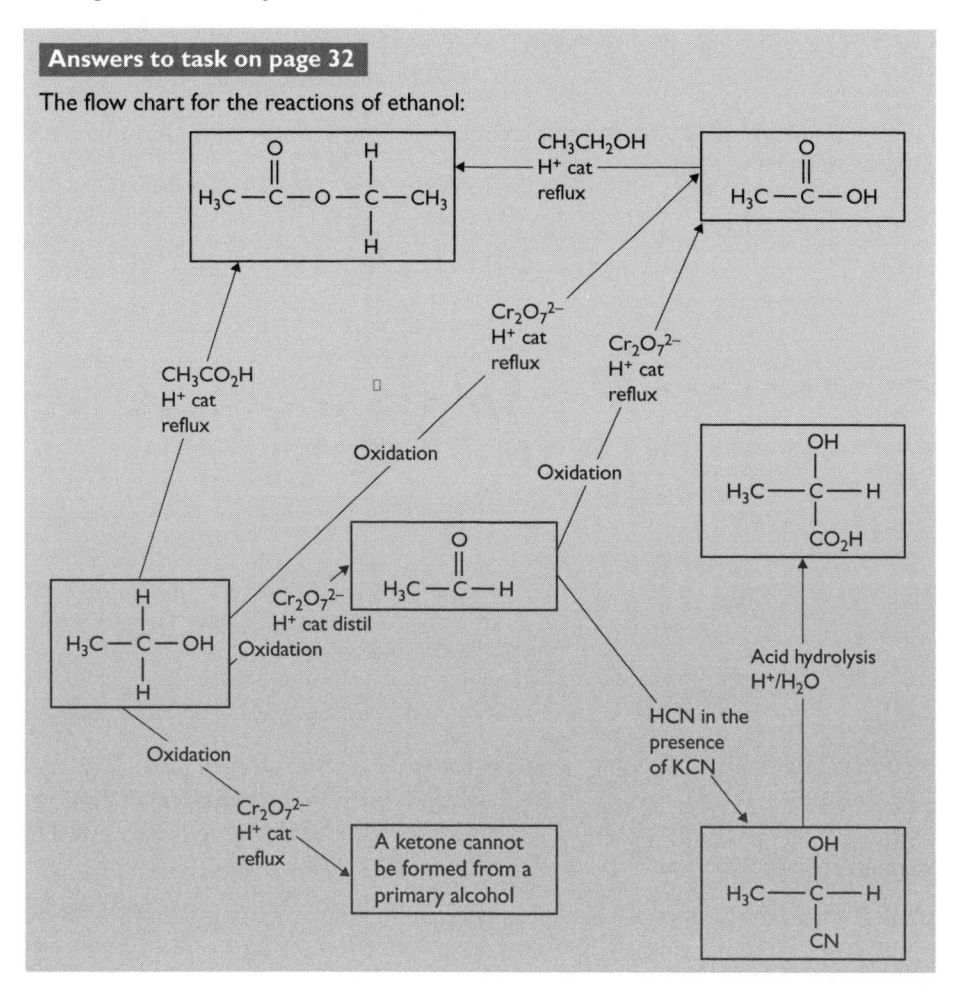

Answers to task on page 32

The flow chart for the reactions of ethanol:

[Flow chart showing ethanol (H₃C—CH(H)—OH) undergoing various reactions:
- Oxidation with Cr₂O₇²⁻/H⁺ cat distil → ethanal (H₃C—CHO)
- Oxidation with Cr₂O₇²⁻/H⁺ cat reflux → ethanoic acid (H₃C—CO₂H)
- With CH₃CO₂H / H⁺ cat reflux → ethyl ethanoate (H₃C—C(=O)—O—CH(H)—CH₃)
- Ethanoic acid + CH₃CH₂OH / H⁺ cat reflux → ethyl ethanoate
- Ethanal + HCN in the presence of KCN → H₃C—CH(OH)—CN
- Acid hydrolysis H⁺/H₂O → H₃C—CH(OH)—CO₂H
- A ketone cannot be formed from a primary alcohol]

Nitrogen compounds

Primary amines

Aliphatic primary amines such as ethylamine, $CH_3CH_2NH_2$, can be prepared by the reaction between a halogenoalkane and ammonia.

$$CH_3CH_2Cl + NH_3 \longrightarrow CH_3CH_2NH_2 + HCl$$

Aromatic primary amines such as phenylamine, $C_6H_5NH_2$, can be prepared by the reduction of nitrobenzene using tin and concentrated hydrochloric acid. The equation for this reaction is shown below ([H] represents the reducing agent):

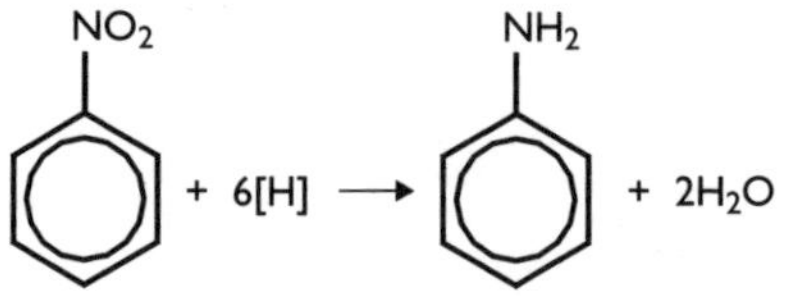

$$C_6H_5NO_2 + 6[H] \longrightarrow C_6H_5NH_2 + 2H_2O$$

Like ammonia, primary amines are weak bases and will accept a proton from water to form an alkaline solution.

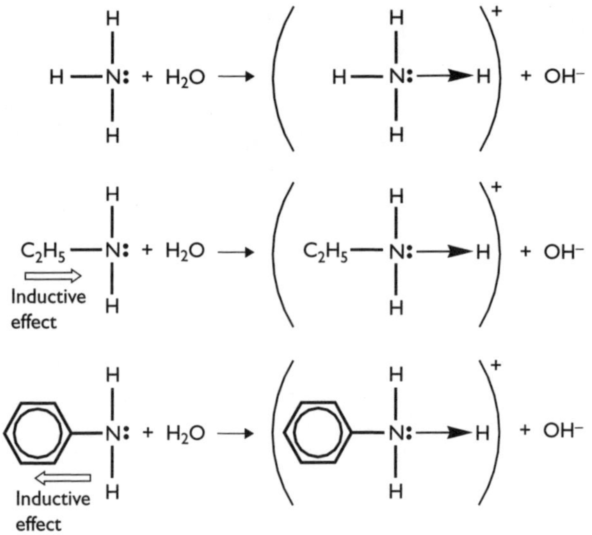

Ammonia and amines have a lone pair of electrons on the nitrogen atom. The lone pair accepts the proton. The base strength depends on the **inductive effect** of the ethyl and phenyl groups. If you are asked to define what is meant by the inductive effect, a suitable definition is *the movement of electrons along a sigma-bond*.

Ethyl groups have a *positive* inductive effect and push electrons along the bond towards neighbouring atoms. This increases the electron density on the N atom and makes ethylamine *more basic*.

OCR Unit 2814

Phenyl groups have a *negative* inductive effect and pull electrons along the bond away from neighbouring atoms. This decreases the electron density on the N atom and makes phenylamine *less basic*. The lone pair of electrons on the N are delocalised into the ring.

The order of basicity is: ethylamine > ammonia > phenylamine.

Primary amines are weak bases and react with acids to produce salts.

$C_2H_5NH_2 + HCl \longrightarrow C_2H_5NH_3^+Cl^-$
Ethylamine

$C_6H_5NH_2 + HCl \longrightarrow C_6H_5NH_3^+Cl^-$
Phenylamine

Aromatic amines, such as phenylamine, are essential for the manufacture of azo dyes. The synthesis involves two stages:
- formation of a diazonium compound
- a **coupling** reaction with a phenol to form the azo dye

Stage 1
Reagents: nitrous acid, HNO_2, formed from $NaNO_2$ and excess HCl
Conditions: temperature below 10 °C
Balanced equation:

$$C_6H_5NH_2 + HNO_2 + HCl \longrightarrow C_6H_5N_2^+Cl^- + 2H_2O$$

Phenylamine + Nitrous acid + Excess HCl → Benzenediazonium chloride + 2H₂O

The reaction has to be kept below 10 °C because benzenediazonium chloride is unstable and reacts readily with water to produce phenol, N_2 and HCl.

Stage 2
Reagent: phenol
Conditions: alkaline solution (in the presence of $OH^-(aq)$)
Balanced equation:

Benzenediazonium chloride + Phenol → Azo dye + HCl

The –N=N– group absorbs light, making azo compounds brightly coloured. The exact colour depends on other substituents on the aromatic rings.

Amino acids

The general formula of an α-amino acid is RCH(NH$_2$)COOH, where R represents the side-chain.

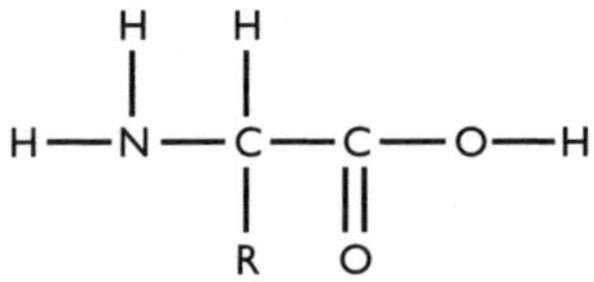

$$H-N(H)-C(H)(R)-C(=O)-O-H$$

The simplest amino acid is aminoethanoic acid, or **glycine**, in which the R group is H. In 2-aminopropanoic acid, or **alanine**, the R group is CH$_3$. These two amino acids are shown below. Alanine has two optical isomers. Glycine is not optically active. Look at the structures — can you explain why?

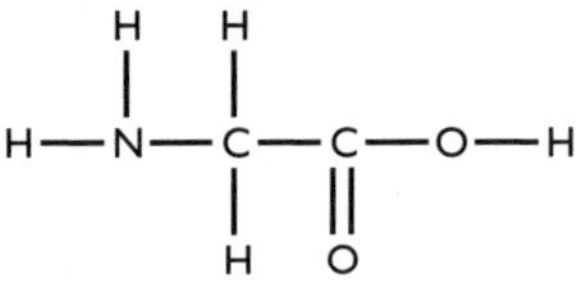

Glycine

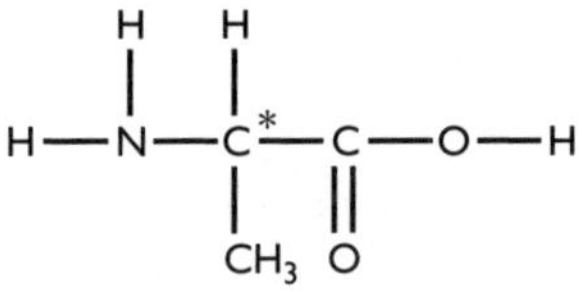

Alanine

Alanine has an asymmetric carbon atom but glycine does not. An asymmetric carbon atom is a carbon atom bonded to four different atoms or groups. Glycine is not optically active because the carbon atom is bonded to two H atoms. The optical isomers of alanine are shown below:

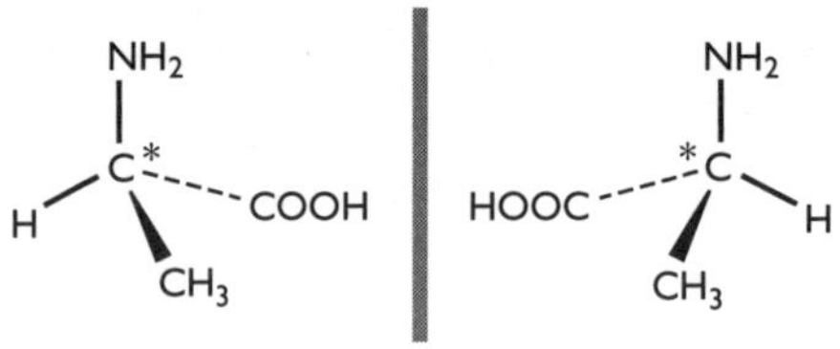

Amino acids are bi-functional because they contain two functional groups — carboxylic acid and amine.

Behaving as a carboxylic acid

An amino acid can react with a base to produce a salt.

CH$_2$NH$_2$CO$_2$H(aq) + NaOH(aq) ⟶ CH$_2$NH$_2$CO$_2^-$Na$^+$(aq) + H$_2$O(l)
   Glycine

An amino acid can react with an alcohol to produce an ester.

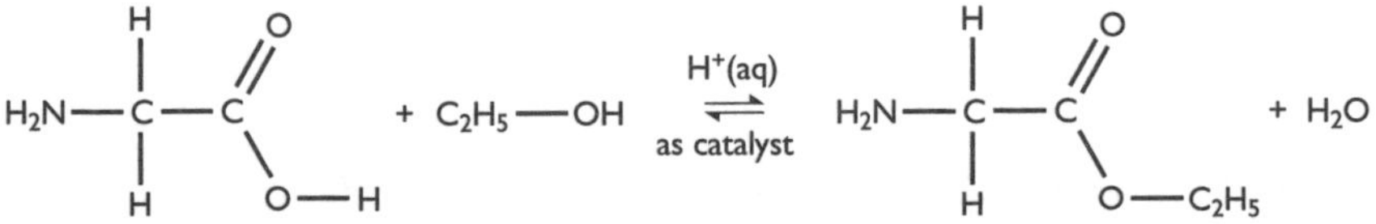

H$_2$N-CH(H)-C(=O)-O-H + C$_2$H$_5$-OH $\rightleftharpoons$ (H$^+$(aq) as catalyst) H$_2$N-CH(H)-C(=O)-O-C$_2$H$_5$ + H$_2$O

Ester

Behaving as a primary amine

An amino acid can react with an acid to produce a salt.

$$HCl + H_2N-CHR-COOH \longrightarrow Cl^- \; H_3N^+-CHR-COOH$$

Properties dependent on both functional groups

Amino acids also display properties that depend on both functional groups. Unlike most organic compounds, amino acids tend to have very high melting points and are water-soluble. This is due to the formation of **zwitterions**.

The amino acid rearranges to form the Zwitterion (with NH_3^+ and COO^-).

The zwitterion for each amino acid exists at a particular pH. The pH at which a zwitterion exists is known as the **isoelectric point**. If the amino acid is in an acidic solution, it forms a cation. If it is in an alkaline solution, it forms an anion.

Cation	Zwitterion	Anion
pH below the isoelectric point	pH at the isoelectric point	pH above the isoelectric point

Amino acids can react to form peptides.

Two amino acids combine with loss of water to form a **peptide link** (–CO–NH–) + H_2O.

If two different amino acids such as glycine (Gly) and alanine (Ala) react, it is possible to form two different dipeptides.

[Diagram showing Gly + Ala → Gly-Ala with loss of water, forming peptide link; and Ala + Gly → Ala-Gly with loss of water, forming peptide link]

All dipeptides can react further with additional amino acids, extending the chain length. This leads to the formation of polypeptides and proteins.

Peptides and proteins can be hydrolysed to the amino acids by refluxing the peptide (or protein) with 6.0 mol dm^{-3} hydrochloric acid.

Polymerisation

There are two categories of polymers: addition polymers and condensation polymers.

Addition polymers

Alkenes can undergo addition reactions in which an alkene molecule joins to others so that a long molecular chain is built up. The individual alkene molecule is a **monomer** and the long chain molecule is a **polymer**.

OCR Unit 2814

Polymerisation can be initiated in a variety of ways and the initiator is often incorporated at the start of the long molecular chain. However, if the initiator is disregarded, the empirical formulae of the monomer and the polymer are the same. Common monomers and the polymers formed from them are shown below:

$$n\ H_2C=CH_2 \rightarrow {-(CH_2-CH_2)_n-}$$
Ethene → Poly(ethene)

$$n\ H_2C=CHCH_3 \rightarrow {-(CH_2-CH(CH_3))_n-}$$
Propene → Poly(propene)

$$n\ H_2C=CHCl \rightarrow {-(CH_2-CHCl)_n-}$$
Chloroethene or vinyl chloride → Poly(chloroethene) or PVC

$$n\ H_2C=CH(C_6H_5) \rightarrow {-(CH_2-CH(C_6H_5))_n-}$$
Phenylethene (styrene) → Polystyrene

It is possible to deduce the repeat unit of an addition polymer from its structure and therefore to identify the monomer from which the polymer was produced. However, when the polymer is drawn to show the correct three-dimensional shape, the resulting structure is crowded and difficult to follow (A, below). This can be simplified either by drawing the skeletal form (B) or by representing the structure as a two-dimensional projection (C).

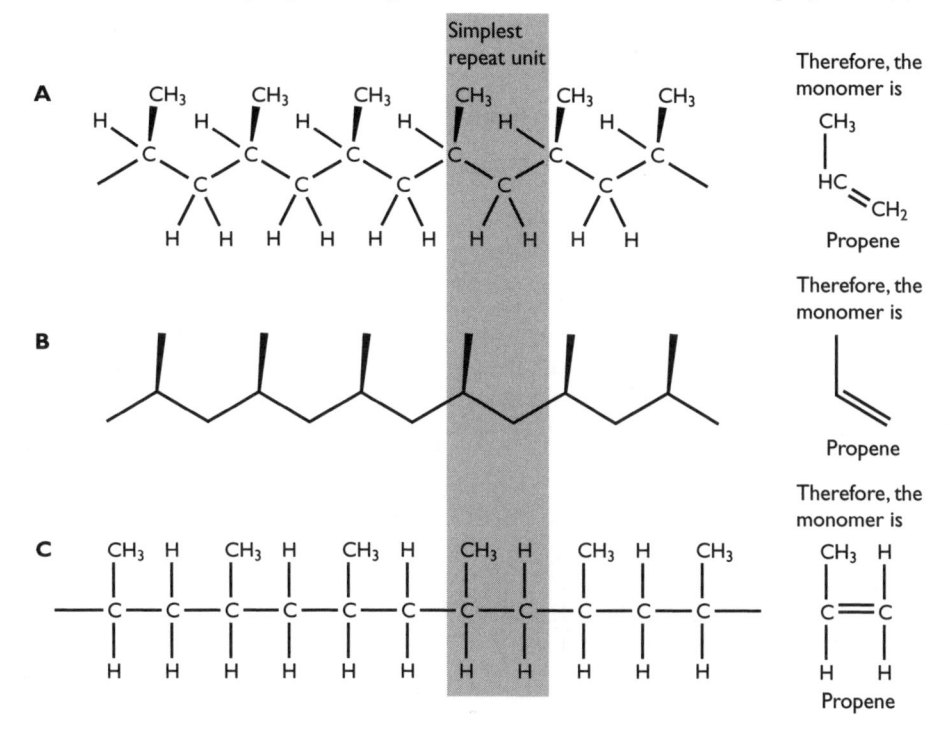

A — three-dimensional representation of poly(propene) chain with CH₃ groups.

Therefore, the monomer is
$$CH_3-HC=CH_2$$
Propene

B — skeletal form of poly(propene).

Therefore, the monomer is propene (skeletal).

C — two-dimensional projection of poly(propene).

Therefore, the monomer is
$$CH_3-CH=CH_2$$
Propene

The bonds in addition polymers are strong, covalent and non-polar, which makes most polymers resistant to chemical attack. Also, they are **non-biodegradable** because they are not broken down by bacteria. The widespread use of these polymers has created a major disposal problem.

Using propene as the monomer, it is possible to prepare three different forms of poly(propene), because alternate carbon atoms along the chain are asymmetric and hence are chiral centres. The easiest way to represent these three forms is by drawing skeletal or two-dimensional representations of the polymers. The three forms are outlined below:

- **Isotactic** — the methyl groups are all on one side of the polymer chain. This gives a regular structure that is rigid, tough and can withstand heat.

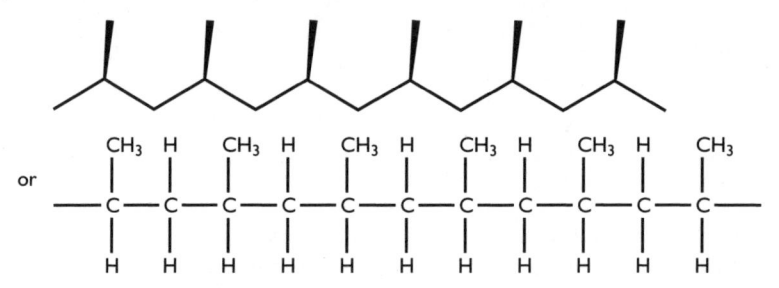

- **Syndiotactic** — the methyl groups alternate between one side of the polymer chain and the other. This also gives a regular structure that is rigid, tough and can withstand heat.

- **Atactic** — the methyl groups are randomly distributed on either side of the polymer chain. This gives an irregular structure that is soft and flexible. The appearance of atactic polymers has resulted in the slang term 'snotty'.

Many other polymers, such as poly(chloroethene), PVC, also exist in three different forms. The isotactic form of PVC is shown below:

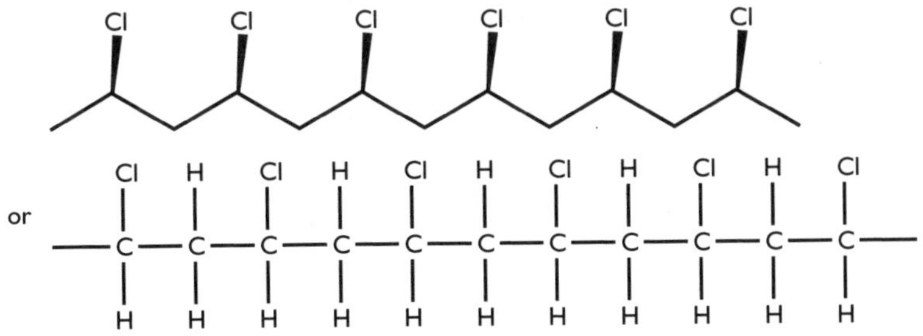

or

Condensation polymers

Condensation polymers are formed when monomers react together and 'condense' out a small molecule such as H_2O or HCl. There are two main types: polyesters and polyamides.

Polyesters

Terylene is a common polyester made by the reaction between the monomers ethene-1,2-diol and benzene-1,4-dicarboxylic acid.

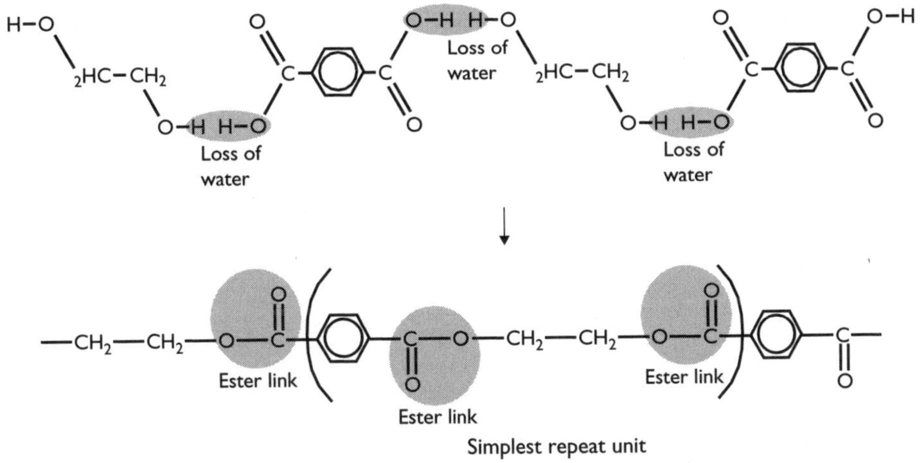

The resulting polymer is almost linear. This means that the polymer chains can be packed closely together. The close packing produces strong intermolecular forces which enable the polymer to be spun into thread.

Polyamides

Polyamides are prepared from two monomers, one with an amine group at each end and the other with a carboxylic acid group at each end. Nylon 6,6 is made from the two monomers 1,6-diaminohexane and hexane-1,6-dicarboxylic acid. It is called nylon 6,6 because each monomer contains 6 carbon atoms.

Nylon forms a strong, flexible fibre when it is melt-spun.

Kevlar is another polyamide. It is stronger than steel and is fire resistant. It is used for making bulletproof vests, crash helmets and protective clothing used by fire fighters. Kevlar is made from two monomers: benzene-1,4-diamine and benzene-1,4-dicarboxylic acid.

There are 20 α-amino acids that occur naturally in the body. They make up a variety of natural polypeptides known as proteins. A peptide (or amide) link is formed between the amine group of one amino acid and the carboxylic acid of another amino acid. Each peptide link is formed by the loss of one water molecule, so proteins are built up in a similar way to nylon and Kevlar. The formation of dipeptides is covered on pages 37–38.

Spectroscopy

Chemists now have a wide range of analytical techniques available for identifying the structure of a compound. You have already met two of these techniques in AS chemistry.

Mass spectrometry

This was introduced in Module 2811: Foundation Chemistry, where it was used to determine the relative atomic mass of elements. In this unit, you are expected to be able to use mass spectrometry to determine the relative molecular mass of a molecule.

The mass spectrum of propan-1-ol is shown below. The mass/charge ratio, m/e, of the molecular ion is 60. The molecular ion is shown by the peak with the highest mass/charge ratio.

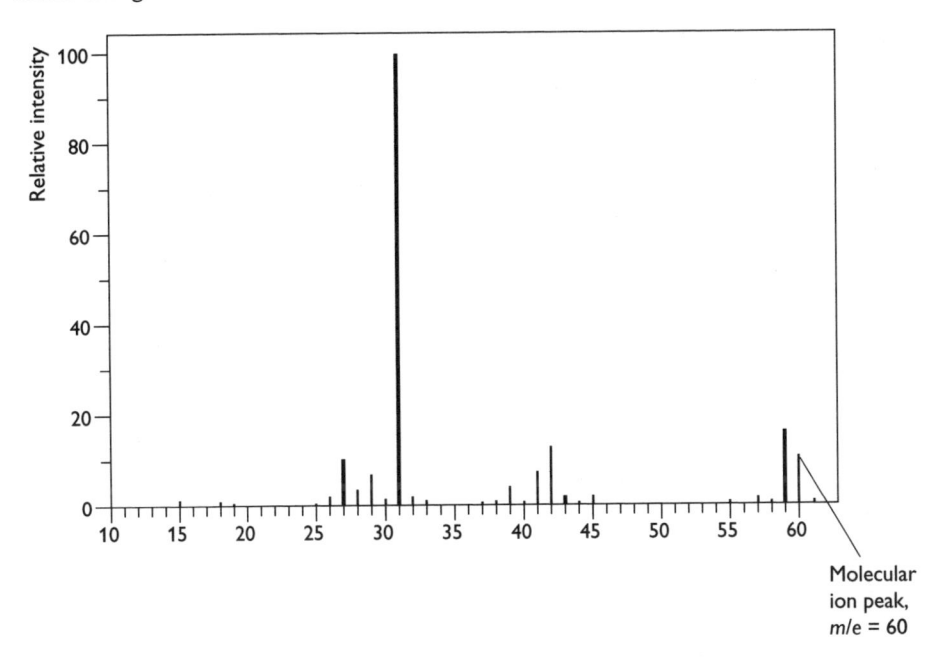

Molecular ion peak, $m/e = 60$

The molecular ion is formed by the molecule losing an electron. This is achieved by bombarding the molecule with high-energy electrons:

$e^- + CH_3CH_2CH_2OH(g) \longrightarrow CH_3CH_2CH_2OH^+(g) + 2e^-$

There are other peaks in the mass spectrum which give further information about the structure. However, all that is required for this unit is the identification of the molecular ion peak and hence the deduction of the relative molecular mass of the compound. Mass spectrometry is studied in greater depth in Module 2815/04: Methods of Analysis and Detection.

Infrared spectroscopy

This was first introduced in Module 2812. Simple infrared spectra enable the identification of functional groups in a molecule. In this module, the groups are limited to alcohols, carbonyls, carboxylic acids and esters.

Compound	Functional group	Absorption
Alcohols	—O—H	3230–3550 cm^{-1}
Carbonyls	—C=O	1680–1750 cm^{-1}
Carboxylic acids	—C(=O)—OH	1680–1750 cm^{-1} 2500–3300 cm^{-1}
Esters	—C(=O)—O—	1680–1750 cm^{-1} 1000–1300 cm^{-1}

Notice that both carboxylic acids and esters have two characteristic absorptions.

Task The four infrared spectra shown below are of propan-1-ol, propanal, propanoic acid and propyl propanoate. Use a *Data Sheet* to identify which is which. The answers are on page 47.

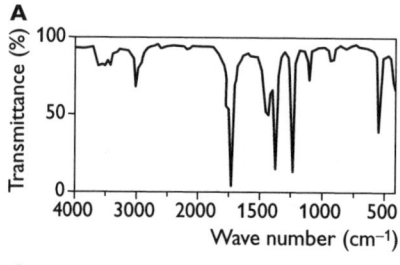

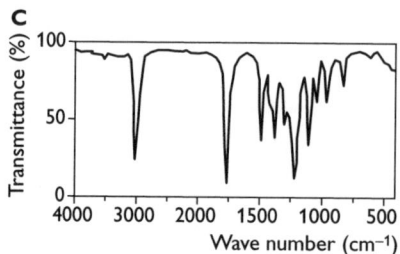

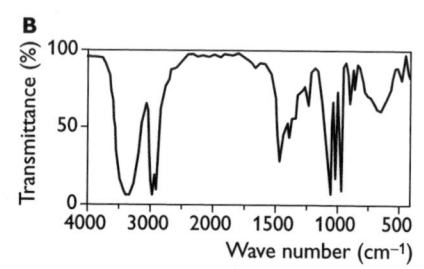

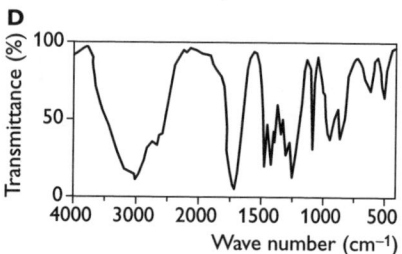

Nuclear magnetic resonance spectroscopy

NMR spectroscopy is a very powerful tool for determining the structure of a compound. In this unit, you are expected to be able to predict and recognise high-resolution NMR spectra of simple organic compounds containing only carbon, hydrogen and oxygen.

If the nucleus of an atom contains an odd number of nucleons (protons and neutrons), it has a net nuclear spin and can be detected using radio frequency. ^{1}H and ^{13}C can both be detected. The radio frequency at which they can be detected varies slightly, depending on the surrounding atoms, i.e. depending on the chemical environment. This slight variation is the key to determining structure and is known as the chemical shift, δ.

It is essential that you are able to recognise different chemical environments. Consider a molecule of ethanol, C_2H_5OH.

$$H-\underset{\underset{H}{|}}{\overset{\overset{H}{|}}{C}}-\underset{\underset{H}{|}}{\overset{\overset{H}{|}}{C}}-OH$$

The six hydrogen atoms are not all identical. The H atoms in the CH_3 group are all in the same environment and can be labelled H_a; so are the H atoms in the middle CH_2 group (labelled H_b). The H in the OH group is different from all of the rest (labelled H_c).

$$H_a-\underset{\underset{H_a}{|}}{\overset{\overset{H_a}{|}}{C}}-\underset{\underset{H_b}{|}}{\overset{\overset{H_b}{|}}{C}}-OH_c$$

The six H atoms in ethanol are in three different environments. Therefore, we would expect the NMR spectrum of ethanol to contain three peaks with different chemical shifts. Each environment is measured relative to TMS, which is used as the standard and has a chemical shift equal to zero. You do *not* have to learn any of these peaks. All relevant absorptions are listed in the *Data Sheet*, which you will be given in the examination.

In the NMR spectrum of ethanol, each peak is a different size. The relative size reflects the number of H atoms in each environment:
- H_a — there are three H atoms in this environment
- H_b — there are two H atoms in this environment
- H_c — there is one H atom in this environment

It follows that the relative intensity of each peak, $H_a:H_b:H_c$, is 3:2:1.

The H atoms attached to one carbon atom influence the H atoms on adjacent carbon atoms. This is called **spin–spin coupling** and results in splitting of the peaks. The easiest way to predict the splitting pattern is to count the number of H atoms on the adjacent carbon atoms and then use the '$n + 1$' rule, where n is the number of hydrogen atoms on the adjacent carbon atoms.

In the NMR spectrum of ethanol, each of the peaks is split differently:
- H_a is attached to a carbon next to the CH_2 group and hence is split into (2 + 1) — a **triplet**.
- H_b is attached to a carbon next to the CH_3 group and hence is split into (3 + 1) — a **quartet**.

- H_c is not attached to a carbon atom and hence does not undergo spin–spin coupling. It is, therefore, a **singlet**.

Hence, we would expect the high-resolution NMR spectrum of ethanol to have three peaks of relative intensity 3:2:1, split into a triplet, a quartet and a singlet. The exact position (the chemical shift) of each peak can be obtained from the data below.

Type of proton	Chemical shift, δ
R—CH$_3$	0.7–1.6
R—CH$_2$—R	1.2–1.4
R$_3$CH	1.6–2.0
—C(=O)—CH$_3$, —C(=O)—CH$_2$—R	2.0–2.9
C$_6$H$_5$—CH$_3$, C$_6$H$_5$—CH$_2$—R	2.3–2.7
—O—CH$_3$, —O—CH$_2$—R	3.3–4.3
R—OH	3.5–5.5
C$_6$H$_5$—OH	6.5–7.0
C$_6$H$_5$—H	7.1–7.7
R—C(=O)—H , C$_6$H$_5$—C(=O)—H	9.5–10
—C(=O)—OH	11.0–11.7

- The –CH$_3$ (H$_a$) has a chemical shift in the range 0.7–1.6 ppm.
- The –CH$_2$– (H$_b$) has a chemical shift in the range 3.3–4.3 ppm.
- The –OH (H$_c$) has a chemical shift in the range 3.5–5.5 ppm.

The NMR spectrum of ethanol is shown below.

OCR Unit 2814

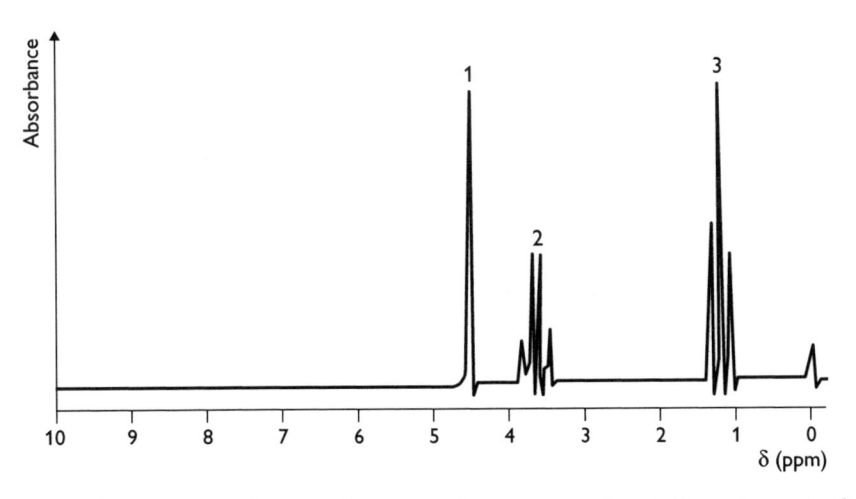

Propan-1-ol and propan-2-ol are isomers. The mass spectra of these isomers show that each has a relative molecular mass of 60. The infrared spectra show that each isomer has an absorption in the region 3230–3550 cm^{-1}, confirming the presence of an –O–H group in each case.

However, the NMR spectra are very different.

Isomer	Number of peaks	Relative intensity	Splitting
H$_a$–C(H$_a$)(H$_a$)–C(H$_b$)(H$_b$)–C(H$_c$)(H$_c$)–O–H$_d$	Four peaks H$_a$:H$_b$:H$_c$:H$_d$	H$_a$:H$_b$:H$_c$:H$_d$ 3:2:2:1	H$_a$ triplet H$_b$ sextet H$_c$ triplet H$_d$ singlet
H$_a$–C(H$_a$)(H$_a$)–C(H$_b$)(O H$_c$)–C(H$_a$)(H$_a$)–H$_a$	Three peaks H$_a$:H$_b$:H$_c$	H$_a$:H$_b$:H$_c$ 6:1:1	H$_a$ doublet H$_b$ septet H$_c$ singlet

Answers to task on page 44

The four infrared spectra shown are:
- **A** = propanal
- **B** = propan-1-ol
- **C** = propyl propanoate
- **D** = propanoic acid

47

Questions & Answers

A2 Chemistry

This section contains questions similar in style to those you can expect to see in Unit Test 2814. The limited number of questions means that it is impossible to cover all the topics and all the question styles, but they should give you a flavour of what to expect. The responses that are shown are real students' answers to the questions.

There are several ways of using this section. You could:
- hide the answers to each question and try the question yourself. It needn't be a memory test — use your notes to see if you can actually make all the points that you ought to make
- check your answers against the candidates' responses and make an estimate of the likely standard of your response to each question
- check your answers against the examiner's comments to see if you can appreciate where you might have lost marks
- take on the role of the examiner and mark each of the responses yourself and then check to see if you agree with the marks awarded by the examiner

The unit test lasts 90 minutes and there is a total of 90 marks. Time is very tight, so it is important that you practise answering questions under timed conditions as part of your revision.

Examiner's comments

All candidate responses are followed by examiner's comments. These are preceded by the icon 🖉 and indicate where credit is due. In the weaker answers, they also point out areas for improvement, specific problems and common errors such as lack of clarity, weak or non-existent development, irrelevance, misinterpretation of the question and mistaken meanings of terms.

Question 1

Addition polymers

Propene is an important industrial chemical essential for the production of a wide range of polymers, plastics and fibres. By far the greatest use of propene is as the monomer polymerised to poly(propene).

(a) (i) Draw the monomer propene. (1 mark)
    (ii) Draw a section of poly(propene) to show *two* repeat units. (2 marks)

(b) There are difficulties caused by waste polymers such as poly(propene). Not only are they non-biodegradable but when burnt they produce a wide range of compounds with toxic fumes, such as acrolein, $CH_2=CHCHO$, which has a choking odour and is the major cause of death by suffocation in house fires. Identify the two functional groups present in acrolein and describe how you could test to show the presence of each group. Describe what you would see with each test. (6 marks)

Total: 9 marks

■ ■ ■

Candidates' answers to Question 1

Candidate A
(a) (i)
$$\begin{array}{c} CH_3 \quad\; H \\ \;|\quad\quad\; | \\ C = C \\ \;|\quad\quad\; | \\ H \quad\;\; H \end{array}$$

Candidate B
(a) (i) $CH_3CH=CH_2$

✎ Both candidates score 1 mark.

Candidate A
(a) (ii)
$$\begin{array}{c} \quad CH_3 \; H \quad\; CH_3 \; H \\ \quad\;|\quad\; |\quad\quad\;|\quad\; | \\ -C-C-C-C- \\ \quad\;|\quad\; |\quad\quad\;|\quad\; | \\ \quad H \quad\; H \quad\;\; H \quad\; H \end{array}$$

Candidate B
(a) (ii)
$$\begin{array}{c} H \; H \; H \; H \; H \; H \\ |\;\; |\;\; |\;\; |\;\; |\;\; | \\ -C-C-C-C-C-C- \\ |\;\; |\;\; |\;\; |\;\; |\;\; | \\ H \; H \; H \; H \; H \; H \end{array}$$

51

🅮 Candidate A scores 1 mark but loses 1 mark carelessly by not showing the fourth bond on the right-hand carbon atom. Candidate B scores no marks because the polymer drawn is poly(ethene) and not poly(propene). This is a common error and one to avoid.

Candidate A
(b) Alkene and aldehyde groups. Alkenes decolourise bromine water. Aldehydes give a silver mirror with Tollen's reagent.

Candidate B
(b) Acrolein contains a carbonyl, which will react with 2,4-dinitrophenylhydrazine to produce a red precipitate. It also contains a C=C, which turns bromine clear.

🅮 Candidate A scores all 6 marks. Candidate B scores 5 out of 6, losing a mark by using the word 'clear' in the test for the alkene. Bromine is a clear solution; it just happens to be a clear brown solution — since it is already clear, it cannot 'turn clear'.

🅮 **Candidate A scores 8 out of 9 marks while candidate B scores 6. Candidate B's overall response to this question is equivalent to a grade C, but with a little care the score could have increased by 1 or 2 marks to the A/B borderline.**

Nitration of arenes

Methylbenzene is an important industrial chemical. It is used in the production of polyurethane plastic foams and fibres such as *lycra*. The production of such foams and fibres involves the nitration of methylbenzene.

(a) Methylbenzene undergoes electrophilic substitution with the nitronium ion, NO_2^+, to form 4-nitromethylbenzene, $CH_3C_6H_4NO_2$.

   (i) With the aid of curly arrows, show the mechanism for the formation of 4-nitromethylbenzene.

                                                                                                                      (3 marks)

   (ii) In a laboratory preparation, 9.20 g of methylbenzene was used and 5.48 g of pure 4-nitromethylbenzene was isolated. Calculate the percentage yield. (5 marks)

(b)

                4-nitromethylbenzene   4-aminomethylbenzene

   (i) Suggest a suitable reducing agent or a suitable reducing mixture for this reaction. (1 mark)

   (ii) Construct a balanced equation for this reduction. Use [H] to represent the reducing agent. (2 marks)

(c) There are six structural isomers of dinitromethylbenzene, $CH_3C_6H_3(NO_2)_2$. Four are drawn for you; draw the structure of the other two isomers.

                                                                                                                           (2 marks)

question 2

A2 Chemistry

(d) The manufacture of *lycra* involves one of these six isomers. A small section of *lycra* is shown below:

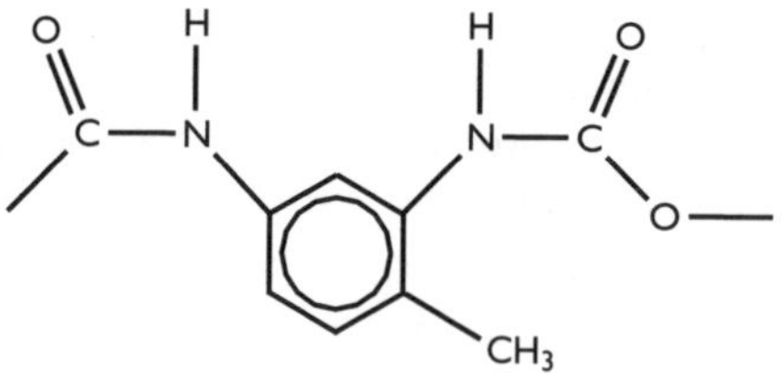

[Structure showing: CH₃C(=O)-NH-(benzene ring with CH₃ substituent)-NH-C(=O)O-]

Draw the structure of the isomer of dinitromethylbenzene used in the manufacture of *lycra*. (1 mark)

Total: 14 marks

■ ■ ■

Candidates' answers to Question 2

Candidate A
(a) (i)

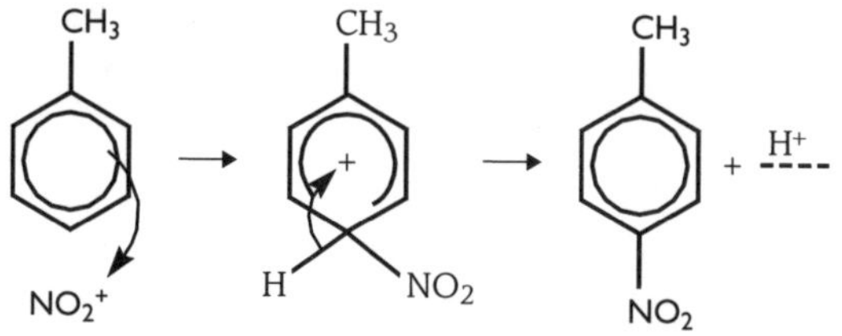

[Mechanism showing electrophilic substitution of NO₂⁺ onto methylbenzene, with intermediate showing broken π ring at attacked carbon, forming nitromethylbenzene + H⁺]

Candidate B
(a) (i)

[Similar mechanism but with curly arrow not starting from the π delocalised ring, and broken π ring drawn over three carbon atoms]

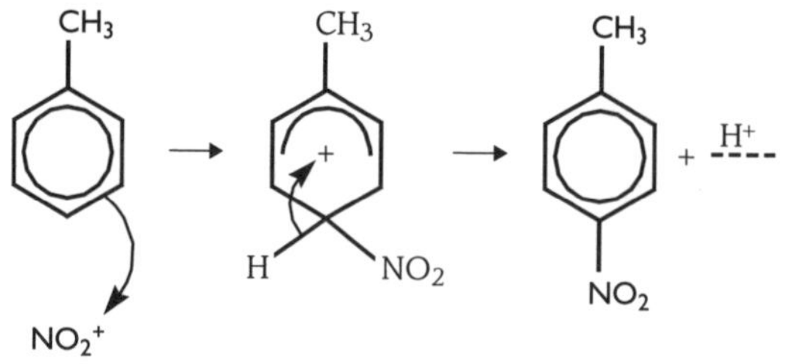

🖉 Candidate A scores all 3 marks but candidate B only scores 1. The first marking point is the curly arrow from the π delocalised ring to the NO_2^+ ion. B's curly arrow doesn't start at the π delocalised ring. The second marking point is the intermediate, which must show clearly the net positive charge and the breaking of the π delocalised ring at the carbon being attacked. Candidate B has carelessly drawn the broken π delocalised ring over three carbon atoms. The final marking point is for the curly arrow showing the reforming of the π delocalised ring. This also results in the formation of H⁺, which must be included to score the mark.

OCR Unit 2814

Candidate A
(a) (ii) Moles of reagent = 9.20/93 = 0.099
Moles of product = 5.48/139 = 0.039
% yield = (0.039/0.099) × 100 = 39.8%

Candidate B
(a) (ii) 40%

✎ Candidate A scores 3 out of 5. The relative molecular masses of both methylbenzene and 4-nitromethylbenzene are incorrect and therefore Candidate A loses two marks. However, full credit is given for the rest of the calculation on the basis of 'error carried forward'. Candidate A has displayed good examination technique and has shown all the working. This enables the examiner to see where mistakes were made and to award marks for the correct processing of the numbers. Candidate B scores all 5 marks for the correct value. However, Candidate B shows poor examination technique by not showing the working. If Candidate A had not shown the working, the score would have been zero.

Candidate A
(b) (i) Sn and concentrated HCl

Candidate B
(b) (i) $LiAlH_4$

✎ Both candidates gain the mark. Candidate A has quoted the reducing agent mentioned in the specification, but $LiAlH_4$ would also work and so earns the mark.

Candidate A
(b) (ii)

CH_3-C_6H_4-NO_2 + 6[H] → CH_3-C_6H_4-NH_2 + $2H_2O$

Candidate B
(b) (ii)

CH_3-C_6H_4-NO_2 —6[H]→ CH_3-C_6H_4-NH_2

✎ Candidate A scores both marks. Candidate B loses 1 mark by forgetting to include water in the equation, which is, therefore, not balanced.

question 2

A2 Chemistry

Candidate A
(c)

[Structure 1: benzene ring with CH₃ (top), O₂N (left), NO₂ (bottom)]

[Structure 2: benzene ring with CH₃ (top), O₂N and NO₂ on meta positions]

Candidate B
(c)

[Structure 1: benzene ring with CH₃ (top), O₂N (upper left), NO₂ (lower right)]

[Structure 2: benzene ring with CH₃ (top), O₂N and NO₂ on meta positions]

e Candidate A scores both marks. Candidate B scores 1 mark only, because the first structure drawn is the same as the third structure given in the question.

Candidate A
(d)

[Structure: benzene ring with O₂N (upper left), NO₂ (upper right), CH₃ (bottom)]

Candidate B
(d) 2,4-dinitromethylbenzene

e Again, candidate A shows good examination technique and scores the mark. Candidate B ignores the question, which instructs the candidates to 'draw the structure' and therefore scores no marks. This is particularly unfortunate because candidate B had named the product correctly.

e Candidate B seems to be a very bright candidate but is perhaps trying to be too clever by cutting corners. This is evident in (a)(ii) when no working is shown. Candidate B scores all the 5 available marks but could easily have lost them all. In the final part, Candidate B does more than is necessary by naming the product but loses the mark by not following the instructions. This means that the candidate had to first deduce the structure and then name it, apparently in their head, since there is no evidence of working. Candidate A shows understanding and carefully uses the information in the question. The net result is that candidate A scores 12 out of 14 marks, a strong grade A answer, while candidate B scores 9, which is borderline C/B grade standard.

Question 3

Carbonyls and carboxylic acids

Propan-1-ol can be oxidised both to propanal and to propanoic acid.

(a) (i) State a suitable oxidising mixture. (2 marks)

(ii) State what you would see during the oxidations. (1 mark)

(iii) Using [O] to represent the oxidising mixture, write a balanced equation to show the conversion of propan-1-ol to propanal. (1 mark)

(iv) Similarly, write a balanced equation to show the conversion of propanal to propanoic acid. (1 mark)

(b) Describe a simple chemical test that would distinguish between propanal and propanoic acid. State what you would see. (2 marks)

(c) Compound **X** has the following percentage composition by mass: C, 62.1; H, 10.3; O, 27.6. The relative molecular mass of compound **X** is 116. Compound **X** can be hydrolysed to form propan-1-ol and propanoic acid. Use *all* the information in the question to deduce the molecular formula of compound **X**. Draw the structure of compound **X**. Show all your working. (6 marks)

Total: 13 marks

■ ■ ■

Candidates' answers to Question 3

Candidate A
(a) (i) Acidified potassium dichromate

Candidate B
(a) (i) $H^+/Cr_2O_7^-$

🖉 Candidate A gains both marks: 1 for the acid and 1 for the dichromate. Candidate B scores the mark for the acid (H^+) but loses the mark for the dichromate because the charge on the ion should be 2–, not 1–.

Candidate A
(a) (ii) Orange to green

Candidate B
(a) (ii) Turns green

🖉 Both candidates gain the mark.

Candidate A
(a) (iii)

H—C(H)(H)—C(H)(H)—C(H)(H)—OH + [O] → H—C(H)(H)—C(H)(H)—C(H)=O

question 3

Candidate B

(a) (iii)

$$CH_3CH_2CH_2OH \xrightarrow{[O]} CH_3CH_2CHO$$

e Neither candidate scores the mark because neither has balanced the equation. This is a very common error. The balanced equation also has water as a product.

Candidate A

(a) (iv)

$$\text{H}_3\text{C-CH}_2\text{-CHO} + [O] \rightarrow \text{H}_3\text{C-CH}_2\text{-COOH}$$

Candidate B

(a) (iv)

$$CH_3CH_2CHO \xrightarrow{[O]} CH_3CH_2COOH$$

e Both candidates score the mark because the equation is automatically balanced.

Candidate A

(b) Add a solution of sodium hydrogencarbonate to both. The propanoic acid will react and you will see bubbles of CO_2. The propanal will not react.

Candidate B

(b) The pH of the acid is lower than the pH of propanal.

e Candidate A gains both marks for describing a suitable chemical test and appropriate observations. Candidate B has described how pH could be used to distinguish between the two chemicals. pH is most easily measured using a pH meter which is not a *chemical* test. Candidate B would probably be awarded 1 mark but may fail to score.

Candidate A

(c)

	C	H	O
Moles	62.1/12 = 5.175	10.3/1 = 10.3	27.6/16 = 1.725
Ratio (divide by smallest)	3	5.97	1

Empirical formula = C_3H_6O which has a mass of 36 + 6 + 16 = 58
Two empirical units (2 × 58 =116) are needed to make the molecular mass.
Therefore, the molecular formula is $C_6H_{12}O_2$.
Compound X is:

$$H_3C-CH_2-CH_2-O-CO-CH_2-CH_3$$

Candidate B

(c) Compound X is propanoate because it hydrolyses to form propan-1-ol and propanoic acid.

$$CH_3CH_2COOCH_2CH_2CH_3 + H_2O \longrightarrow CH_3CH_2COOH + CH_3CH_2CH_2OH$$

🖉 The marking points are: correct empirical formula ✓; empirical mass = 58 ✓; showing that two empirical units are needed ✓; correct molecular formula ✓; using propan-1-ol and propanoic acid to deduce which isomer of $C_6H_{12}O_2$ is compound X ✓; identifying propyl propanoate ✓. Candidate A has been very methodical and followed the guidelines given in the question, scoring 5 out of 6 marks. The only thing missing is an explanation of how he/she deduced that the isomer of $C_6H_{12}O_2$ is propyl propanoate. Candidate B is clearly very able but has not followed the instructions in the question. He/she gains the mark for the correct molecular formula and the mark for using propan-1-ol and propanoic acid to deduce which isomer of $C_6H_{12}O_2$ is compound X. The mark for 'drawing' propyl propanoate is also awarded because the formula used is unambiguous. Candidate B scores 3 out of 6 marks.

🖉 **As an examiner it is possible to feel a great deal of sympathy for Candidate B. Clearly, the candidate has a good understanding of the topic. However, poor examination technique results in consistent under-achievement. This is particularly evident in part (c) where Candidate B quickly sees the answer and correctly deduces the identity of compound X, but doesn't follow the instructions in the question to use *all* of the information given. Consequently, Candidate B only scores 7 out of a possible 13 marks, which equates to a grade C/D. By contrast, Candidate A is much more methodical and scores a grade A mark of 11 out of 13.**

Amino acids

This question is about the amino acids shown in the table below.

Key	Name	Structure
Ala	Alanine	H₂N–CH(CH₃)–COOH
Gly	Glycine	H₂N–CH₂–COOH
Phe	Phenylalanine	H₂N–CH(CH₂C₆H₅)–COOH
Cys	Cysteine	H₂N–CH(CH₂SH)–COOH

(a) A dipeptide is hydrolysed into its amino acids and the amino acids are identified by chromatography. The results are shown on the chromatogram below.

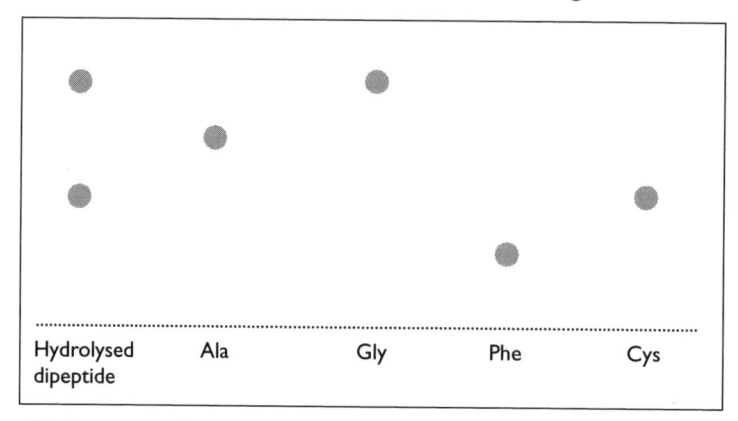

(i) Identify the *two* amino acids present in the dipeptide. (1 mark)

(ii) Suggest *two* possible structures of the dipeptide. (2 marks)

(b) The pH at which the zwitterions of glycine, alanine and phenylalanine exist are:
- glycine, 6.0

OCR Unit 2814

- alanine, 6.0
- phenylalanine, 5.5

(i) Draw the ions formed by glycine at pH = 6.0, alanine at pH = 10.0 and phenylalanine at pH = 2.0. (3 marks)

(ii) Suggest why a solution of glycine does *not* conduct electricity at pH = 6.0. (1 mark)

(iii) Suggest why a solution of alanine does conduct electricity at pH = 10.0. (1 mark)

Total: 8 marks

■ ■ ■

Candidates' answers to Question 4

Candidate A
(a) (i) Glycine and cysteine

Candidate B
(a) (i) Gly and Cys

☒ Both candidates gain the mark.

Candidate A
(a) (ii) [structures of two dipeptides shown, with CH₂SH side chains]

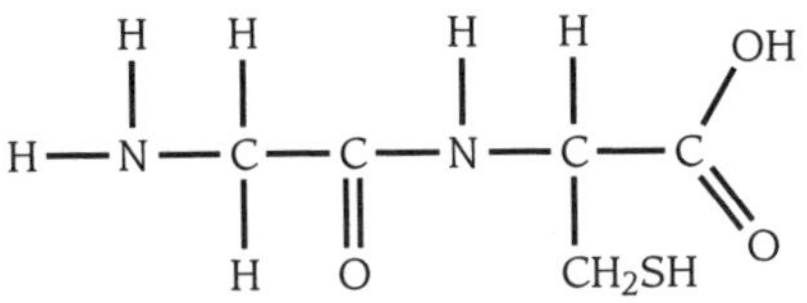

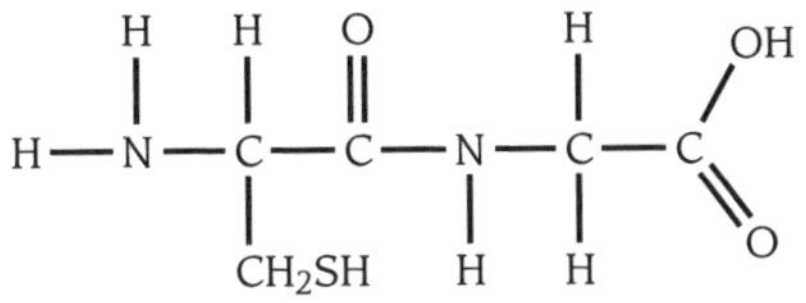

Candidate B
(a) (ii) [structure of one dipeptide shown, with CH₂SH side chain]

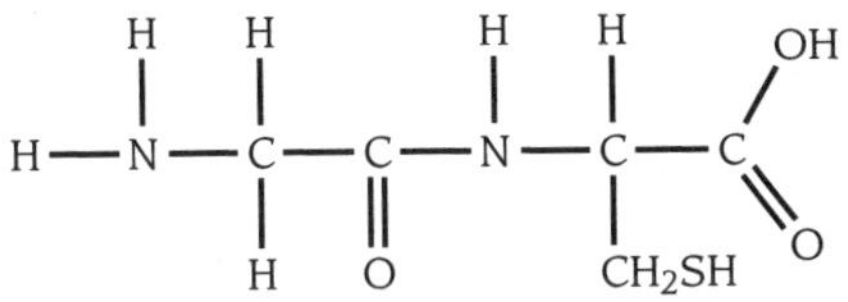

☒ Candidate A gains both marks. However, Candidate B has not read the question and only drawn one of the two dipeptides, for 1 mark.

Candidate A
(b) (i) [structures shown for pH = 6.0 (glycine zwitterion), pH = 10.0 (alanine with NH₂ and COOH, CH₃ side chain), and pH = 2.0 (phenylalanine with NH₃⁺ and COO⁻, CH₂C₆H₅ side chain)]

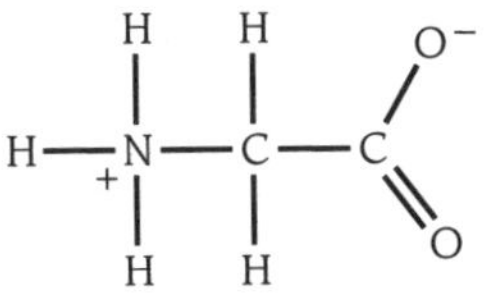

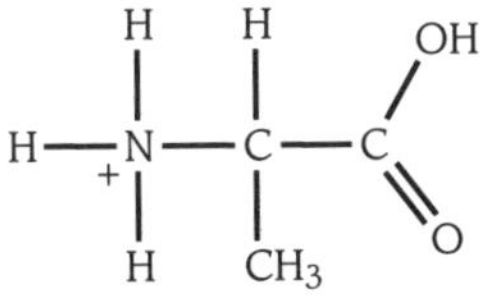

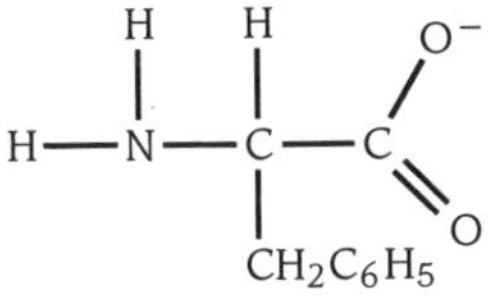

A2 Chemistry

Candidate B
(b) (i)

pH = 6.0 H—N(H)(H+)—C(H)(H)—C(=O)(O⁻)

pH = 10.0 H—N(H)(H)—C(H)(CH₃)—C(=O)(O⁻)

pH = 2.0 H—N(H)(H+)—C(H)(CH₂C₆H₅)—C(=O)(OH)

e Candidate A scores 1 mark for the zwitterion at pH = 6.0. However, the charges on the other two ions are incorrect. Candidate B gains all 3 marks.

Candidate A
(b) (ii) The zwitterion has no net charge.

Candidate B
(b) (ii) It is a poor conductor.

e Candidate A gains the mark. Candidate B has simply restated the question and is awarded no marks.

Candidate A
(b) (iii) The ion is positive and therefore moves to the cathode.

Candidate B
(b) (iii) It is a good conductor.

e Candidate A gains the mark. Candidate B has made the same mistake as in part (b)(ii) and scores nothing.

e The most difficult part of this question is (b)(i). Overall, Candidate A scores **6 marks out of 8** and Candidate B scores **5**.

Question 5

Organic synthesis

(a) Consider the reaction scheme shown below:

$$H-\underset{}{C}=O \xrightarrow{\text{Step 1}} H-\underset{CN}{\overset{CH_3}{\underset{|}{C}}}-OH \xrightarrow{\text{Step 2}} H-\underset{CO_2H}{\overset{CH_3}{\underset{|}{C}}}-OH \xrightarrow{H^+/Cr_2O_7^{2-}} \text{Compound } C$$

Compound **B**

(i) State the reagent(s) that could be used for step 1. (1 mark)
(ii) State the reagent(s) that could be used for step 2. (1 mark)

(b) Compound B, lactic acid, is found in cheese. It can exist as two optical isomers.
(i) What structural feature in compound B causes optical isomerism? (1 mark)
(ii) Suggest why compound B, prepared by the reaction scheme outlined above, would *not* be optically active. (1 mark)

(c) (i) Draw the structure of compound C. (1 mark)
(ii) Compound C can be reduced to propane-1,2-diol. Using [H] to represent the reducing agent, construct a balanced equation for this reaction. (3 marks)

Total: 8 marks

■ ■ ■

Candidates' answers to Question 5

Candidate A
(a) (i) HCN

Candidate B
(a) (i) HCN

✎ Both candidates gain the mark.

Candidate A
(a) (ii) Dilute sulphuric acid

Candidate B
(a) (ii) H⁺(aq)

✎ Both candidates gain the mark.

Candidate A
(b) (i) Compound B contains an asymmetric carbon atom that is bonded to four different atoms or groups.

Candidate B
(b) (i) It has mirror images.

# question 5

> 🅔 Candidate A scores the mark but Candidate B does not. It is true that optical isomers form mirror images, but the key feature is that the mirror images are *non-superimposable*.

Candidate A

(b) (ii) It forms a mixture.

Candidate B

(b) (ii) An equal amount of each isomer is formed and therefore they cancel each other out.

> 🅔 Candidate B shows good understanding and gains the mark. Candidate A is on the right lines but needs to explain that a synthetic preparation usually produces a mixture containing 50% of each isomer. This mixture is known as a racemic mixture and is optically inactive.

Candidate A

(c) (i)

$$\text{H}-\underset{\underset{\text{CO}_2\text{H}}{|}}{\overset{\overset{\text{CH}_3}{|}}{\text{C}}}=\text{O}$$

Candidate B

(c) (i)

$$\underset{\underset{\underset{\text{H}}{|}}{\overset{\|}{\text{C}}=\text{O}}}{\overset{\overset{\text{CH}_3}{|}}{\overset{|}{\text{C}}=\text{O}}}$$

> 🅔 Neither candidate scores the mark. It is important to recognise that the functional group attached to the middle carbon atom is a secondary alcohol and will therefore be oxidised to a ketone. The other functional group is a carboxylic acid, which is not oxidised. Both candidates recognise that the alcohol will be oxidised. However, Candidate A loses the mark because the central carbon atom has five bonds. Candidate B loses the mark because the carboxylic acid has been reduced back to an aldehyde. The correct structure is:

$$\underset{\underset{\text{CO}_2\text{H}}{|}}{\overset{\overset{\text{CH}_3}{|}}{\text{C}}}=\text{O}$$

OCR Unit 2814

Candidate A

(c) (ii)

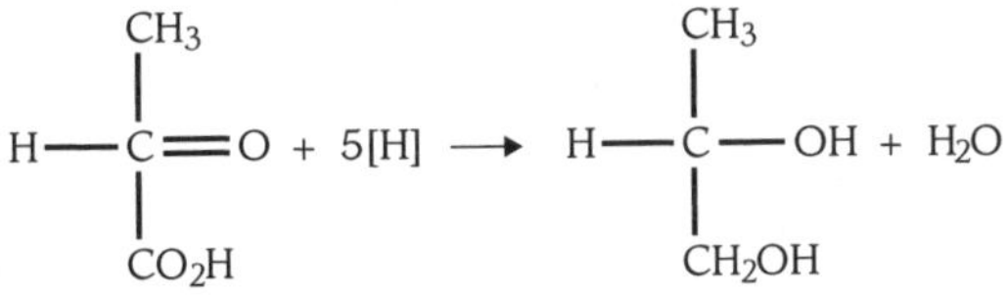

$$\begin{array}{c} CH_3 \\ | \\ H-C=O \\ | \\ CO_2H \end{array} + 5[H] \longrightarrow \begin{array}{c} CH_3 \\ | \\ H-C-OH \\ | \\ CH_2OH \end{array} + H_2O$$

Candidate B

(c) (ii)

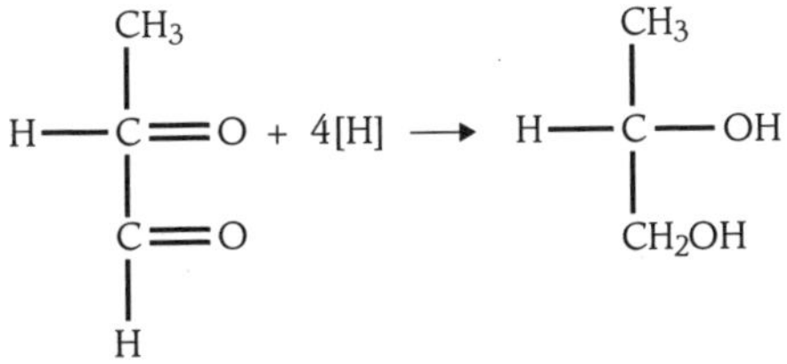

$$\begin{array}{c} CH_3 \\ | \\ H-C=O \\ | \\ C=O \\ | \\ H \end{array} + 4[H] \longrightarrow \begin{array}{c} CH_3 \\ | \\ H-C-OH \\ | \\ CH_2OH \end{array}$$

e The three marking points for this part are: correct formula for propane-1,2-diol ✓; H_2O as a product ✓; the equation correctly balanced ✓. Candidate A scores 2 marks and Candidate B scores 1. The correct equation is:

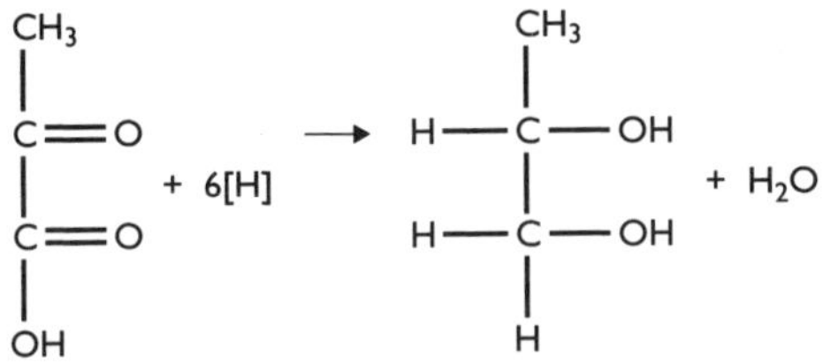

$$\begin{array}{c} CH_3 \\ | \\ C=O \\ | \\ C=O \\ | \\ OH \end{array} + 6[H] \longrightarrow \begin{array}{c} CH_3 \\ | \\ H-C-OH \\ | \\ H-C-OH \\ | \\ H \end{array} + H_2O$$

Compound C   Propane-1,2-diol

e This is a difficult question. Candidate A scores 5 out of 8 marks and Candidate B scores 4. Questions like this are often asked. Examiners are able to use unfamiliar molecules to test routine functional group chemistry. The key to answering this type of question successfully is to identify the essential functional groups and, in each case, to concentrate on the chemistry of the group, ignoring the rest of the molecule.

Carboxylic acids, esters and aldehydes

Compound A has the structure shown below:

HO—CH$_2$—CH$_2$—O—C(=O)—C$_6$H$_4$—C(=O)—OH

(a) (i) Deduce the molecular formula of compound A. (1 mark)
   (ii) Calculate the empirical formula of compound A. (1 mark)
(b) Compound A can undergo (i) oxidation, (ii) hydrolysis and (iii) neutralisation. Complete the schemes below by stating the reagent(s) and conditions, if any. Draw the structure for each organic product.
   (i) Oxidation of compound A
      • Reagents:
      • Conditions:
      • Organic product(s): (3 marks)
   (ii) Hydrolysis of compound A
      • Reagents:
      • Conditions:
      • Organic product(s): (4 marks)
   (iii) Neutralisation of compound A
      • Reagents:
      • Organic product(s): (2 marks)

Total: 11 marks

Candidates' answers to Question 6

Candidate A
(a) (i) C$_{10}$H$_{10}$O$_5$

Candidate B
(a) (i) HOCH$_2$CH$_2$OOCC$_6$H$_4$COOH

e Candidate A is correct, for 1 mark. Candidate B does not gain the mark because molecular formulae should always be written in the form C$_x$H$_y$O$_z$, with the elements that make up the compound grouped together.

Candidate A
(a) (ii) C$_2$H$_2$O

OCR Unit 2814

Candidate B

(a) (ii) C₂H₂O

🅔 Both candidates gain the mark.

Candidate A

(b) (i) Reagents: Cr₂O₇²⁻(aq)
Conditions: H⁺(aq)
Organic product(s):

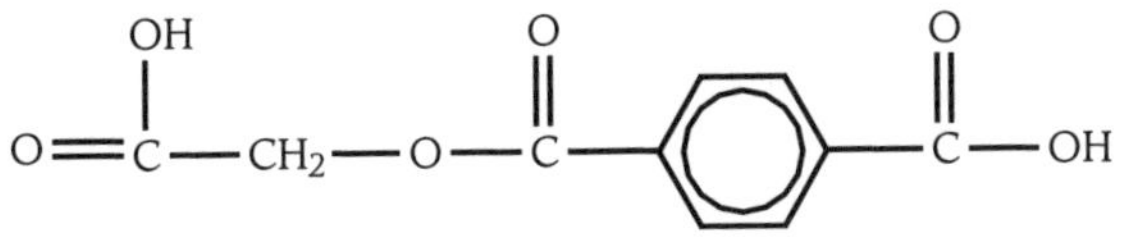

$$O=\overset{OH}{\underset{}{C}}-CH_2-O-\overset{O}{\underset{}{C}}-\langle C_6H_4 \rangle-\overset{O}{\underset{}{C}}-OH$$

Candidate B

(b) (i) Reagents: dichromate
Conditions: heat
Organic product(s):

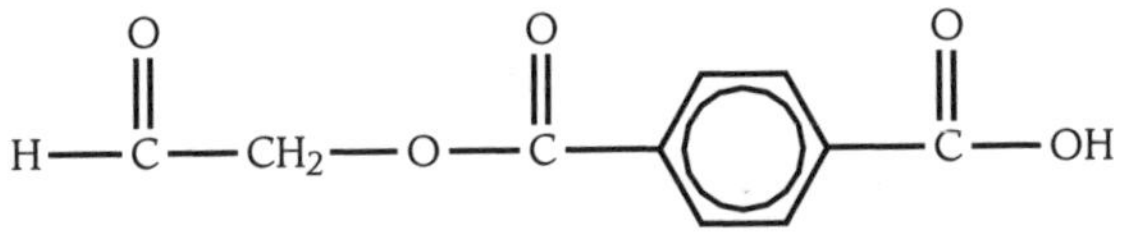

$$H-\overset{O}{\underset{}{C}}-CH_2-O-\overset{O}{\underset{}{C}}-\langle C_6H_4 \rangle-\overset{O}{\underset{}{C}}-OH$$

🅔 Candidate A scores all 3 marks. Candidate B loses a mark by not stating that the dichromate must be acidified. The functional group oxidised is a primary alcohol and therefore the product could be either a carboxylic acid (see Candidate A's answer) or an aldehyde (see Candidate B's response).

Candidate A

(b) (ii) Reagents: H₂SO₄
Conditions: heat
Organic product(s):

HO—CH₂—CH₂—OH and HO—C(=O)—⟨C₆H₄⟩—C(=O)—OH

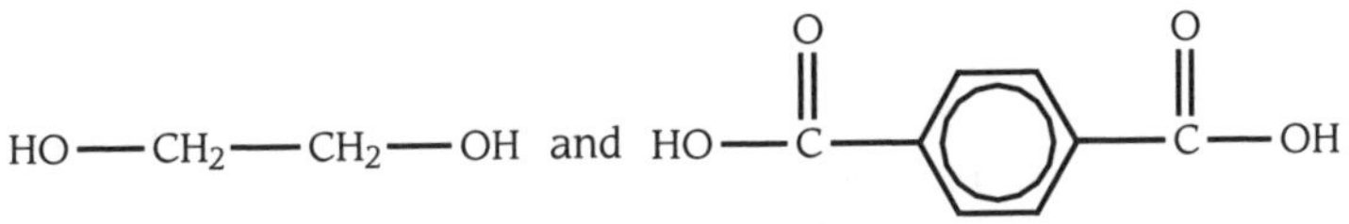

Candidate B

(b) (ii) Reagents: NaOH(aq)
Conditions: heat
Organic product(s):

HO—C(=O)—⟨C₆H₄⟩—C(=O)—OH and HO—CH₂—CH₂—OH

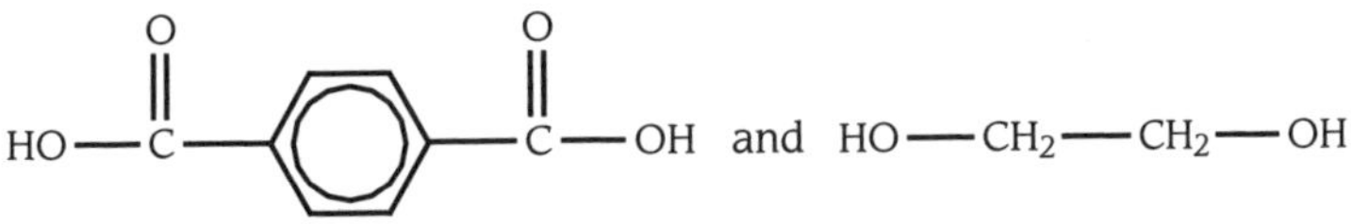

question 6

> Candidate A scores 3 out of 4 marks. The reagents/conditions must include water. If Candidate A had written dilute H_2SO_4 or $H_2SO_4(aq)$, all 4 marks would have been scored. Candidate B also scores 3 marks. A mark is lost because the organic product is not benzene-1,4-dioic acid; it is the sodium salt of the dioic acid. If a base catalyses the hydrolysis, the organic acid produced reacts with the base to produce a salt:

$$Na^+ \; {}^-O-\underset{\underset{O}{\|}}{C}-C_6H_4-\underset{\underset{O}{\|}}{C}-O^- \; Na^+$$

> This is a difficult marking point. If you are allowed to select the catalyst, it is always safer to choose an acid.

Candidate A

(b) (iii) Reagents: NaOH(aq)
Organic product(s):

$$Na^+ \; {}^-O-CH_2-CH_2-O-\underset{\underset{O}{\|}}{C}-C_6H_4-\underset{\underset{O}{\|}}{C}-O^- \; Na^+$$

Candidate B

(b) (iii) Reagents: NaOH(aq)
Organic product(s): H_2O

> Both candidates score 1 mark. Candidate A is almost correct. However, only the carboxylic acid reacts in a neutralisation reaction; the primary alcohol is unaffected by a base. Candidate B is hoping that there is an easy mark to pick up, but hasn't read the question carefully enough. The question asks for the 'organic product', so water earns no marks.

> This is another difficult question, making use of functional group chemistry in an unfamiliar situation. Candidate A has done very well, scoring an A-grade mark of 9 out of 11. Candidate B has scored 7 marks, equivalent to a C grade, but with more care could have gained the mark lost in (a)(i) and with a little more learning would have known that the dichromate oxidising agent has to be acidified. Every mark is important! The 2 extra marks would have transformed Candidate B's answer from grade C to grade A standard.

Question 7

Amides, esters and chirality

Aspartame, shown below, can be used as an artificial sweetener.

$$H_2N-CH(CH_2CO_2H)-C(=O)-N(H)-CH(CH_2C_6H_5)-C(=O)-O-CH_3$$

(a) (i) Aspartame contains five functional groups, including the benzene ring. Name the other *four* functional groups. (4 marks)

(ii) *Two* of the four functional groups can be hydrolysed. Circle these groups on the diagram above. (2 marks)

(iii) Show the structures of the organic products formed by the complete hydrolysis of aspartame. (3 marks)

(b) (i) Aspartame has two chiral carbon atoms. Identify each with an asterisk (*) on the diagram above. (2 marks)

(ii) Explain what is meant by the term *chiral*. (1 mark)

(c) Aspartame can be made from aspartic acid (shown below).

$$H_2N-CH(CH_2CO_2H)-C(=O)-OH$$

(i) Aspartic acid also has a chiral carbon atom. Draw its optical isomers. Suggest the value of the bond angles around the chiral carbon atom. (3 marks)

(ii) Suggest the structure of a compound that could react with aspartic acid to make aspartame. (1 mark)

Total: 16 marks

■ ■ ■

Candidates' answers to Question 7

Candidate A
(a) (i) Amide, carboxylic acid, ester, peptide

Candidate B
(a) (i) Amine, amide, ketone, carboxylic acid, ester

question 7

e Candidate A gains 3 of the 4 marks. 1 mark is lost because amide and peptide are the same. The missing functional group is **amine**. Many candidates adopt the technique used by Candidate B. The question asks for *four* functional groups, so candidates think they are hedging their bets by listing *five* functional groups. There are *only four* functional groups. By writing five, Candidate B automatically loses 1 mark. The wrong answer is marked first — the examiner will not select the correct answers from a list of alternatives.

Candidate A
(a) (ii)

Candidate B
(a) (ii)

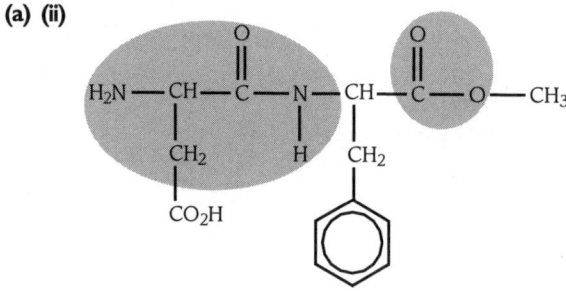

e Candidate A scores both marks. Candidate B loses a mark by extending the circle to include both the amide and amine groups.

Candidate A
(a) (iii)

OCR Unit 2814

Candidate B
(a) (iii)

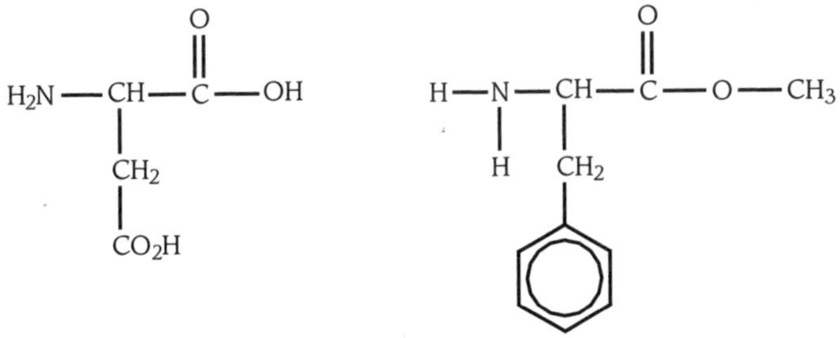

$$H_2N-CH(CH_2CO_2H)-C(=O)-OH \qquad H-N(H)-CH(CH_2C_6H_5)-C(=O)-O-CH_3$$

🖉 There are 3 marks allocated here, indicating clearly that there are three products. Candidate A has used this information but Candidate B displays poor examination technique by only drawing two products. Hydrolysis is a difficult concept and both candidates only score 1 out of 3 marks. Both the amide and the ester undergo hydrolysis. The bonds that break and the correct products are shown in the diagram below. Use this answer to work out where each candidate went wrong.

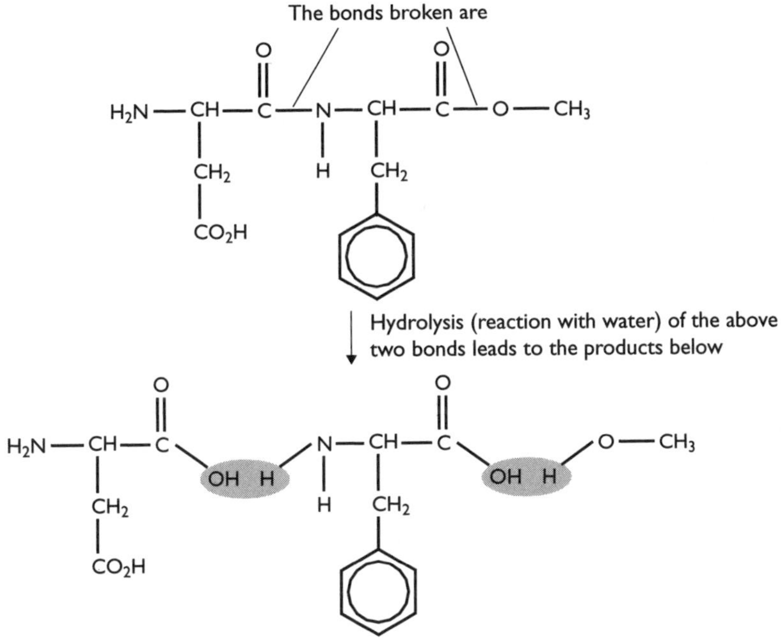

The bonds broken are

$$H_2N-CH(CH_2CO_2H)-C(=O)\diagup N(H)-CH(CH_2C_6H_5)-C(=O)\diagup O-CH_3$$

Hydrolysis (reaction with water) of the above two bonds leads to the products below

$$H_2N-CH(CH_2CO_2H)-C(=O)-\boxed{OH\ H}-N(H)-CH(CH_2C_6H_5)-C(=O)-\boxed{OH\ H}-O-CH_3$$

For any hydrolysis reaction, the key features to look out for are the ester group and the amide (peptide) group. Both groups undergo hydrolysis:

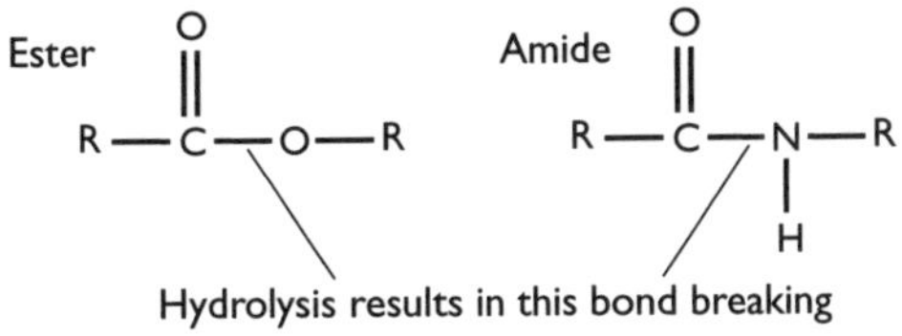

Ester: $R-C(=O)\diagup O-R$ Amide: $R-C(=O)\diagup N(H)-R$

Hydrolysis results in this bond breaking

71

question 7

Candidate A
(b) (i)

H₂N—*CH—C(=O)—N—*CH—C(=O)—O—CH₃
         | | |
         CH₂   H   CH₂
         | |
         CO₂H   (phenyl ring)

Candidate B
(b) (i)

H₂N—*CH—C(=O)—N—CH—C(=O)—O—CH₃
         | | |
         CH₂   H   CH₂
         | |
         CO₂H   (phenyl ring)

> Candidate A gains both marks. Candidate B has ignored the instructions in the question and only identified one of the chiral carbons, for 1 mark.

Candidate A
(b) (ii) The carbon is bonded to four different atoms or groups.

Candidate B
(b) (ii) Bonded to four atoms or groups.

> Candidate A scores the mark but Candidate B carelessly loses the mark. Carbon atoms are often bonded to four atoms or groups — the key point missed by Candidate B is that the four atoms or groups are all *different*.

Candidate A
(c) (i)

         NH₂   NH₂
          | ,,H   H,, |
          C   C
   HOOC   CH₂COOH   CH₂COOH   COOH

Bond angle = 109° 28'

Candidate B
(c) (i)

          NH₂   NH₂
       H,, | 109.5° | ,,H
          C   C
   CH₂COOH   COOH   HOOC   CH₂COOH

> Both candidates score all 3 marks.

OCR Unit 2814

Candidate A

(c) (ii) [This was left blank]

Candidate B

(c) (ii)

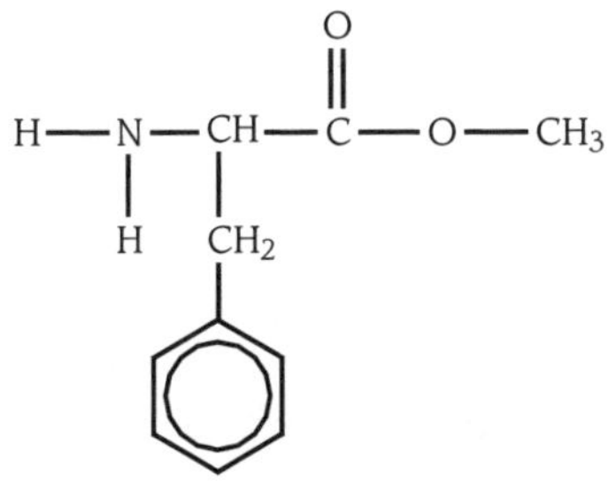

$$\text{H}-\text{N}-\text{CH}-\overset{\displaystyle\overset{\text{O}}{\|}}{\text{C}}-\text{O}-\text{CH}_3$$
$$\phantom{\text{H}-}\ \ |\phantom{-\text{N}-}\ |$$
$$\phantom{\text{H}-}\ \text{H}\phantom{-\text{N}-}\text{CH}_2$$
$$\phantom{\text{H}-\text{N}-\text{CH}-}|$$
$$\phantom{\text{H}-\text{N}-\text{CH}-}\text{C}_6\text{H}_5$$

🖉 Candidate A has made no attempt at this part whereas Candidate B has used the information given in the question and deduced correctly the structure of the compound. Writing nothing will definitely get no marks, so always have a try.

🖉 **Candidate B's response to the final part demonstrates ability and understanding, yet his/her overall score for the question is 10 out of 16 marks, while Candidate A scores 12. Candidate A makes good use of the information in the question and follows the instructions carefully. By contrast, Candidate B often ignores the directions given. Look back at Candidate B's responses and identify where careless errors were made.**

Question 8

Basicity and azo dyes

(a) (i) Explain the relative basicity of ammonia, ethylamine and phenylamine. (5 marks)
   2 marks are available for the quality of written communication. (2 marks)
   (ii) Phenylamine can be converted into benzenediazonium chloride, $C_6H_5N_2Cl$.
   State the reagents and conditions. Write an equation for the reaction. Show
   the structure of benzenediazonium chloride. (5 marks)
(b) Benzenediazonium chloride reacts with a chlorinated phenol to form an azo dye
with a relative molecular mass of 267 and the following composition by mass:
C, 53.9%; H, 3.0%; N, 10.5%; Cl, 26.6%; O, 6.0%. Use this information to deduce the
structure of the azo dye. (4 marks)

Total: 16 marks

■ ■ ■

Candidates' answers to Question 8

Candidate A

(a) (i) A base is defined as a proton acceptor. However, in order to accept a proton the base must have a lone pair of electrons. The relative basicity of the amines is dependent on the availability of the lone pair of electrons on the nitrogen. Availability is influenced by the inductive effects of the alkyl and aryl groups. The ethyl group has a positive inductive effect and pushes the lone pair away from the nitrogen, making it easier to accept a proton. The benzene ring has a negative inductive effect and the lone pair is pulled into the ring, making it more difficult to accept a proton. The order of increasing basicity is:

   phenylamine < ammonia < ethylamine

Candidate B

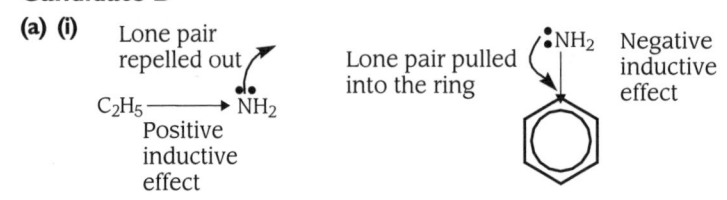

(a) (i) Lone pair repelled out
$C_2H_5 \longrightarrow NH_2$
Positive inductive effect

Lone pair pulled into the ring

NH_2 Negative inductive effect

Ethylamine is more basic than ammonia, which is more basic than phenylamine.

🖉 The marking points are: a base is a proton acceptor ✓ which depends on the ability to donate a lone pair of electrons ✓; alkyls have a positive inductive effect ✓; aryls have a negative inductive effect ✓; order of basicity is $C_2H_5NH_2 > NH_3 > C_6H_5NH_2$ ✓. There are also 2 marks for the quality of written communication. 1 mark is allocated for continuous prose, i.e. two or more consecutive sentences, and the other is for the

OCR Unit 2814

use of correct chemical terms, including **proton acceptor**, **lone pair of electrons** and **inductive effect**. The two candidates have elected to answer in very different ways. Candidate A uses continuous prose and writes all the answer in sentences. Candidate B uses the bare minimum of words and explains the relative basicities using formulae and symbols. The best examination technique is a compromise between the two. It is not always easy to explain chemical phenomena in words and equations; symbols or mechanisms are often better. However, if marks are available for quality of written communication, it is essential to use some continuous prose. Candidate A gives a perfect answer and scores all 7 marks. Candidate B clearly understands the concept but only scores 5 marks. There is no mention of the need to accept a proton and no attempt to write in continuous prose.

Candidate A
(a) (ii) Reagents: sodium nitrate and hydrochloric acid
Conditions: excess HCl(aq); the temperature must be below 10°C

$C_6H_5NH_2 + HNO_2 + HCl \rightarrow C_6H_5NN^+Cl^-$

Candidate B
(a) (ii) $C_6H_5NH_2 + HNO_2 + HCl \rightarrow C_6H_5{}^+N_2Cl^- + 2H_2O$

✍ Candidate A shows good examination technique, but only scores 2 marks, for correctly stating the conditions. The reagents are sodium nitrite (or sodium nitrate(III), $NaNO_2$) and HCl, which in turn produce nitrous acid, HNO_2. No marks are awarded for the equation because Candidate A has forgotten to include the water. The structure of the diazonium chloride is incorrect with the + charge written on the wrong N atom. Candidate B shows poor examination technique by failing to state the reagents and conditions. However, the equation is correct and it also shows that an excess of HCl is required, so 2 marks are awarded. The structure of the diazonium chloride is ambiguous and it is not clear which of the nitrogen atoms is positively charged. The correct structure for the diazonium chloride is:

$C_6H_5\overset{+}{N}NCl^-$

75

question 8

Candidate A
(b)

	C	H	N	Cl	O
Moles	53.9/12 = 4.5	3.0/1 = 3.0	10.5/14 = 0.75	26.6/35.5 = 0.75	6.0/16 = 0.375
Ratio (divide by smallest)	12	8	2	2	1
Mass of element in compound	144	8	28	71	16

Mass of compound = 144 + 8 + 28 + 71 + 16 = 267
Therefore, the empirical and molecular formulae are both $C_{12}H_8N_2Cl_2O$.

Candidate B
(b) $C_{12}H_8N_2Cl_2O$

Both candidates score 3 marks. Candidate B successfully deduces the structure of the azo dye (the most difficult part of the question) while Candidate A makes no attempt to do so. Candidate A demonstrates good examination technique, showing all working. Candidate B calculates the empirical formula, but does not use the relative molecular mass (267) to show that the molecular formula is the same as the empirical formula.

Candidate B seems to understand more of the chemistry than Candidate A and yet only scores 10 out of 16 marks, compared with a score of 12 by Candidate A. Check Candidate B's answers carefully and see if you can spot where poor examination technique has cost marks.

Question 9

Spectroscopy

Compounds A and B are structural isomers.

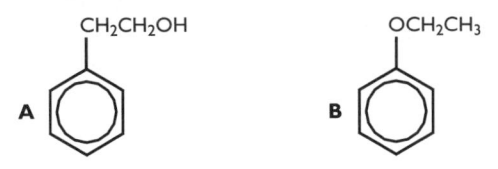

A: benzene ring with CH₂CH₂OH substituent

B: benzene ring with OCH₂CH₃ substituent

(a) (i) Write an equation to show the formation of the molecular ion for compound A. (1 mark)
   (ii) Calculate the mass:charge ratio, m/e, for the molecular ion peak in the mass spectrum of A. (1 mark)
   (iii) What is the molecular formula of these isomers? (1 mark)
(b) A sample of B was analysed to determine its percentage by mass of carbon and hydrogen. Calculate the expected %C and %H. (2 marks)
(c) One of the compounds A or B gives the infrared spectrum below:

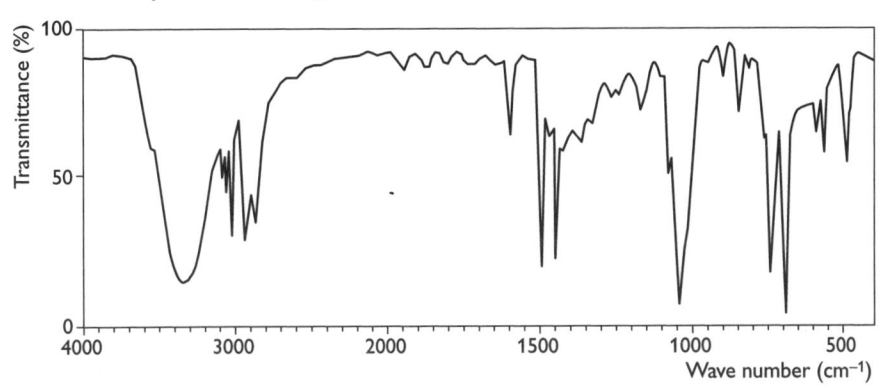

[Infrared spectrum: Transmittance (%) vs Wave number (cm⁻¹), ranging from 4000 to 500 cm⁻¹]

Using the data sheet, identify which of the two compounds A or B has this spectrum. Explain your reasoning carefully. (3 marks)

(d) One of the compounds A or B gives the NMR spectrum below:

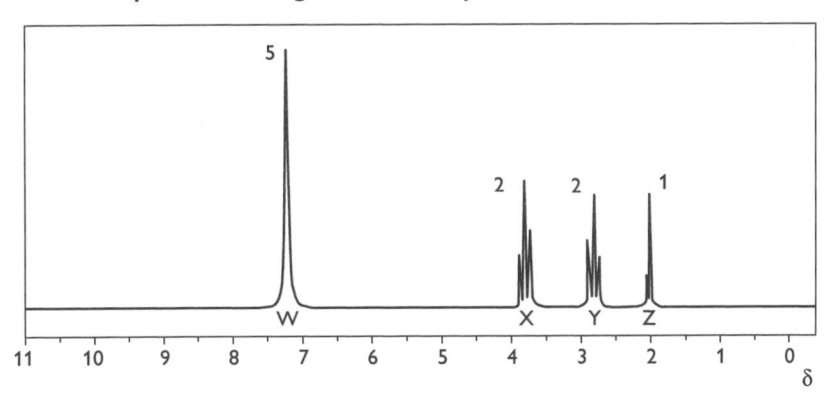

[NMR spectrum with peaks: W (integration 5) at ~7 δ, X (integration 2) at ~4 δ, Y (integration 2) at ~3 δ, Z (integration 1) at ~2 δ; δ axis from 11 to 0]

77

question 9

(i) When a second spectrum was run with D₂O added, the peak Z, at δ 2.0 disappeared. Using the *Data Sheet*, suggest the identity of the protons responsible for the groups of peaks W, X, Y and Z. For each group of peaks, explain your reasoning carefully. Use *all* of the information given. (9 marks)
1 mark is available for the quality of written communication. (1 mark)

(ii) Identify which of the two compounds **A** or **B** has this spectrum. (1 mark)

Total: 19 marks

■ ■ ■

Candidates' answers to Question 9

Candidate A
(a) (i) C₆H₅—CH₂CH₂OH → C₆H₅—CH₂CH₂O⁻ + H⁺

Candidate B
(a) (i) C₆H₅—CH₂CH₂OH + e → (C₆H₅—CH₂CH₂OH)⁺ + 2e

e Candidate B scores the mark, but Candidate A has misunderstood the process of forming the molecular ion, and scores nothing.

Candidate A
(a) (ii) 77 + 14 + 14 + 17 = 122

Candidate B
(a) (ii) 122

e Both candidates are correct, for 1 mark, but Candidate A has shown better exam technique by including some working.

Candidate A
(a) (iii) $C_8H_{10}O$

Candidate B
(a) (iii) $C_6H_5CH_2CH_2OH$

e Candidate A gains the mark but Candidate B does not. Molecular formulae must always be written in the simplest form: $C_xH_yO_z$, where *x*, *y* and *z* are the total numbers of atoms of each element in the molecule.

Candidate A
(b) Carbon: 8 × 12 = 96/122 = 78.7%
    Hydrogen: 10/122 = 8.2%

OCR Unit 2814

Candidate B

(b) C = 78.7%, H = 8.2% and O = 13.1%

🅔 Both candidates score 2 marks. However, Candidate B again shows poor examination technique. In any calculation, you should always show your working. Candidate B also gives the percentage of oxygen, which is not asked for. If it were incorrect, Candidate B might have lost a mark.

Candidate A

(c) The peak between 3230 cm^{-1} and 3550 cm^{-1} is due to the hydrogen bonded –OH group in an alcohol. Therefore, the spectrum is for compound A.

Candidate B

(c) It is the alcohol.

🅔 Candidate A gives the perfect answer, making use of the instructions in the question and quoting directly from the *Data Sheet*. Candidate B is awarded 1 mark for identifying that the spectrum shown is for an alcohol, but loses 2 marks for not giving a reason and not identifying the alcohol as either compound A or B.

Candidate A

(d) (i) When the spectrum is re-run using D$_2$O, peak Z disappears, showing that peak Z is due to a labile proton which is found in groups such as the –OH group. Peaks X and Y are both split into triplets, showing that the adjacent carbons must be attached to two hydrogens — (n + 1) rule. The relative amount of each peak is 2, suggesting that peaks X and Y are both CH$_2$ groups. Peak W is due to the five hydrogens on the benzene ring.

Candidate B

(d) (i) The integration areas of the peaks are 5:2:2:1

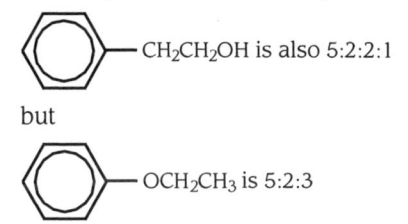

⬡—CH$_2$CH$_2$OH is also 5:2:2:1

but

⬡—OCH$_2$CH$_3$ is 5:2:3

🅔 The marking points are: peak W — benzene ring ✓; chemical shift = 7.1–7.7 ppm *or* relative number of hydrogens is 5 ✓. Peaks X and Y — both are CH$_2$ ✓; relative number of hydrogens is 2 ✓; both are split into triplets ✓; adjacent carbons are attached to 2 hydrogens ✓. Peak X — CH$_2$ attached to the benzene ring ✓; Peak Z — OH ✓; relative amount is 1 *or* when re-run in D$_2$O it disappears ✓; labile ✓. The quality of written communication mark is awarded for the correct use of at least two terms from: labile, integration, chemical shift or splitting. Chemical shift is particularly difficult to assign with any certainty. The values given on the *Data Sheet* are typical values and can vary slightly depending on the solvent, the concentration and, more importantly, the chemical environment. Candidate A follows the guidelines given in the question and scores a total of 10 marks. Try marking Candidate A's answer and see if you can identify which 2 marks have been lost. Candidate B clearly understands NMR and uses it to identify the correct compound, but ignores most of the question. This poses a real dilemma for the examiner. The marker has to stick to the agreed mark scheme and it is just about possible to award Candidate B 3 marks for using the information on the spectrum relating to relative amounts. However, the candidate has ignored the splitting and has not referred to the *Data Sheet*, has not followed the instructions and has not identified which group is responsible for any of the four peaks.

Candidate A

(d) (ii) The NMR spectrum is for compound A.

Candidate B

(d) (ii) It is compound A.

e Both candidates score the mark.

e **This question has been a disaster for Candidate B. He/she clearly understands the work almost as well as Candidate A, but the outcomes could not be more different. Candidate A scores 18 out of 19 marks, which is grade-A standard. Candidate B only scores 9 marks, which is equivalent to a grade D/E. If Candidate B had used the information and then followed the instructions in the question, the overall mark could have been improved dramatically. Copy out Candidate B's answer and identify where poor examination technique loses marks. If you can learn to recognise mistakes made by others, it should be possible to avoid making the same errors yourself.**